BETTER THAN YOU FEEL

Drenda Keesee

Better Than You Feel
Making Your Emotions Work For You

ISBN: 978-0- 9729035-8-5

CONTENTS

INTRODUCTION

The invisible world is where the visible originates. Are you fully persuaded God can do what He said he would do? Most of us would say, "Sure!" But the reality is few people find their way to enjoying the good life we see offered in the promises of God's Word. WHY? There is a reason! And when you understand and unlock some crucial keys, you can prosper and be in health as your *soul* prospers!

When we hear a motivational message or read a promise from God's Word, we can get excited and feel as if anything is possible. We can renew our mind to God's Word and begin to think like He thinks, that all things are possible. The parable of the sower speaks of receiving the Word with joy, BUT when persecution, or we could say people with an opposing view or circumstances come, we can be moved to feel as if it's impossible.

Your feelings play a huge role in whether or not you are able to actually go from thinking success to harnessing your emotions to make them work for you—to make it through the difficulties of life and to realize the success you've dreamed of.

In my book, *Better Than You Think*, I shared the

process to renew the mind and how important it is to know God's thoughts (His Word) about life and how it is to be lived. His thoughts are higher than ours and will bring success. But just as important as it is to *think* His thoughts, we must learn how to make *emotions* or *feelings* work for us and not against us. Many people hear the promise and see the opportunity for success in a business endeavor, marriage relationship or ministry, but when trouble comes, they lose heart or they get emotionally moved to quit or act out of feelings instead of the truths that bring freedom and success.

1 Thessalonians 5:23 says, "May God himself, the God of peace, sanctify you through and through. May your whole spirit, soul and body be kept blameless at the coming of our Lord Jesus Christ."

If you want peace and provision, becoming sanctified or separated is the pathway. <u>The generic meaning of sanctification is "the state of proper functioning."</u> To sanctify someone or something is to set that person or thing apart for the use intended by its designer. So many believers miss that they are spirit, soul and body. They focus only on the new birth spiritually and allow Christ to work there in the born-again experience but neglect to allow God's Spirit to sanctify them in the realm of the soul, as I Thessalonians encourages us. They continue to live in the realm of the thoughts or emotions that they were ruled by *before* Christ's change, neglecting attention to their soul and body. When a person is born again, their spirit is *sanctified*. There is nothing that can be added to the finished work of Christ to make a person any more new spiritually. It's nothing we can earn or work for, but it is based on Christ's work. We are born again, or we call it "the new birth."

So if a person is born anew and begins an exciting journey of faith, why is it that too often we see them fall short of becoming the example of God's promised success—success that is tangible and speaks of a life that was drastically changed? They fail to realize they have a part to play in the area of the soul realm: the mind, will and emotions.

This is a topic we have to address because for so many, their spiritual walk is stifled by their physical desires or emotional tantrums. The Bible says our spirit is willing, but our flesh is weak. Our spirit has been justified through the sacrifice of Jesus Christ. When you're born again your spirit is made blameless, but the problem is in our souls. If we don't know how to manage our mind, will *and emotions*, emotional outbursts sabotage our successes, lead us around on whims, and hold us hostage when we're called to be free.

1 Thessalonians charges us to be blameless not only in our spirit, but also in our soul and body. So what does that look like? How can we manage all three together: our spirit, soul and body? How can we overcome the emotions that lead us blindly through life and make them work *for* us instead of *against* us?

It's possible! And not only is it possible, it's promised!

POSITIVE EMOTIONS

Chapter 1

Leave Your Bags at the Door

A while back I was speaking at a women's conference, and as I stepped up to begin and looked across the auditorium, I found a room full of scowling women with their arms crossed. I hadn't said a word yet, but they seemed resolute to be unhappy. The leaders who invited me to speak acted inconvenienced by the whole event, and as soon as the session started, they slipped to the back. I could feel the emotional suppression over the room—the women were emotionally burned out by circumstances, offenses and pain. They were defeated believers with no joy, no peace or provision. I later discovered that many of them were physically sick as well. To anyone coming in from the outside, it was a terrible representation of God and what being a believer in Christ looks like. Few young women were present because the older women had chased them away with their fears, frowns, furrowed brows and folded arms.

If we live in a place of hurt, how can we be effective in our own lives or in impacting others?

I knew God had a word of encouragement for those women. The more they pouted, the more passionately I preached. A righteous anger came over me—not toward the ladies, but at Satan who wanted to keep them held captive by their attitudes. My instincts would have been to try to appease the women, but the Holy Spirit began to speak through me. Proverbs 27:5 tells us, "Open rebuke is better than secret love" (KJV). Sometimes you have to confront the enemy of negativity, bad attitudes and emotional strongholds keeping people hostage. God loves us too much to leave us the way we are.

I sincerely asked them, "Who wants what you have?" They scowled at me, and it honestly could not have been more unsightly if I had been staring down against an evil spirit. I said, "If we don't have a life of joy, if there's nothing in our life that's admirable, if there's no peace, there's no happiness, who would want our life or our faith? Even if you're going through something, you can smile and fight with some joy. If people don't see that, why would they want what we have?"

The Holy Spirit began speaking to me, "My people have been born again, but they're stopping there. They're not going to the next level with Me. My Spirit is attractive to those who see it." Nobody would want what those women had. There are people who are born again, but they're not experiencing God's freedom, peace, joy and provision.

The Lord began to speak I Thessalonians 5:23 to me over and over, "Now may the God of peace Himself sanctify you completely." The word *sanctify* jumped out with emphasis as I repeated it.

Do you know you can serve God and not be sanctified *completely*? You can be sanctified in the sense that you have been born again in your spirit, but you haven't gone past that. The verse goes on to say, "And may your whole spirit, soul and body be preserved blameless at the coming of our Lord Jesus Christ." May the God of peace sanctify you—spirit, *soul* and body. Some of us are not having the success God wants us to have because we've only sanctified our spirits; we haven't worked on our souls: our mind, will and emotions.

The Lord began to download things to me as I was speaking to the women. I confronted the walls spiritually, and I kept pouring the Word of God out like emptying a pitcher, washing them with the water of the Word and challenging the things in their life. After I spoke at the first session, I went into the bathroom and I prayed every devil-busting prayer I knew. Pacing and fervently praying, I said firmly, "Devil, I take authority over this atmosphere. This is not your atmosphere, because I'm here and the Bible says wherever I put my feet, whatever I possess, it's mine and I take this territory now. I bind you from these women, this situation and from this church!" And then I came out, and nicely and softly said, "Hi ladies, nice to see you. It's so great to be here."

There was a night-and-day difference between the first session and the next. By the end of that session, 90 percent of the women came forward for prayer. Women were crying, laying hands on each other and hugging. You could feel God's Spirit healing women all over the room.

There was an intimidating atmosphere from the get-go trying to push me and my daughters back and keep us from administering God's truth to bring the women out of that thick cloud of oppression. I could have easily quit or preached half-heartedly. There were multiple opportunities to get offended, or to let my emotions run away with feelings of inadequacy. And quite honestly, that's how I would have reacted as a young woman when insecurity and the fear of failure were my defaults. Because

I kept my emotions in check, at the end of the day the women were laughing and praising God passionately. It went from a horror movie to a comedy. I'm serious!

There are people who have been nursing hurts and wounds for years, and any time they begin to see success, the enemy pulls them back into fear, discouragement and causes them to lose the joy of their salvation. Without the joy of our salvation we're not that much, right? It's called the *good news* of the gospel. If it doesn't look like good news, who's going to want it? God is good all of the time, and our life and our attitude should reflect that...not to mention how your attitude and emotional outbursts could be negatively impacting your relationships, business and overall success in life.

Emotions aren't a bad thing. They give us the energy, zeal or warnings that promote action. God created our emotions, and they are a part of our soul. However, if we allow our soul to run wild, it will continually sabotage our success, damage relationships, and bring negative impact to our family and finances. Many start on the pathway to success as a new creation in Christ, only to revert back to negatively programmed thought patterns and picking up emotional baggage that Christ came to set them free from. It's like starting down a beautiful road to a new life and running into a roadblock that we created ourselves. Anger, guilt, offenses and unforgiveness can build walls around your life that keep you from enjoying all of the wonderful benefits of knowing God. You can still get to heaven with an unsanctified soul, but you miss out on the blessings of following Him here, and more importantly, others following Him because of your life. I'm so glad we get what Jesus deserves instead of what we deserve! But to enjoy that gift requires our cooperation. How do we move past baggage and bondage into complete freedom?

Kick-starting Emotions

Emotions are a gift God gave us to enjoy, and a powerful tool that inspires action in us and in others. Your emotions inspire you to act every day, even if you're not aware of it. For example, many hotels offer an incentive to attend a meeting with one of their salespeople, with the hopes of selling you one of their timeshares. On one trip Gary and I took with our young family, we agreed to meet with their salespeople in exchange for four free Disney

World tickets. We warned the man over the phone that we wouldn't be buying their timeshare, but he told us if we listened, we could have the tickets either way. What we walked into was an emotionally compelling, carefully constructed dialogue that provokes people to make rash, impulsive decisions. The speech was built wholly on feelings, not on facts or figures. It would have to be, because financially the investment didn't make sense. The salesman expounded on the luxury of vacationing, the impact it would have on our marriage, how it would make my children want to spend more time with me, and eventually how it would affect my grandchildren. He pulled out all of the stops. When his speech was finished, and we politely declined, his emotional direction changed.

"How could you waste my time like this? I have children and I'm trying to make a living!" he said heatedly.

"I'm sorry, we told you before we started that we weren't going to buy one," Gary said.

The salesman was irate. He tried to guilt us into purchasing one, blame us, accuse us and press us to make the sale. He threatened that we wouldn't get our Disney World tickets if we didn't. When nothing we said seemed to get through to him, Gary pulled out a piece of paper and said, "Let me show you why we're *not* going to do this." He laid out the finances, and in the end, the numbers showed the obvious conclusion that it was a terrible investment. We received our Disney World tickets and left. I felt like I had experienced every emotion in one hour. And if it weren't for my husband's financial expertise, we probably would have walked away from that meeting with a timeshare. Feelings are powerful!

There's a reason commercials, negotiators and politicians speak to us emotionally. Great leaders and marketing companies have learned this principle: *Feelings are kick-starters that inspire us into action.*

Step 1: Use emotions as kick-starters to persuade and motivate yourself and the people around you to act.

People are more likely to make impulse decisions based on their emotions—even if the decision doesn't make sense. In politics, people are inclined to show up to the polls and vote if there is a driving emotion—*hate* toward the opposing candidate's beliefs, *anger* toward injustice, *love* for country, or *fear* of war. So how do we use our emotions to kick start us in the right direction?

Free to Feel

It is for freedom that Christ has set us free. We aren't called to a life of bondage of our soul with its appetites, lusts and emotional baggage. You are created with potential. You have a heart full of treasures—the desires, feelings, talents and unique traits that make you a special individual. What are you doing with them?

KEYS TO WINNING

RIGHT PICTURE
Concept: Faith
Source: God's Word

"Change the Picture"

MORE POWER
Concept: Grace
Source: God's Spirit

"Receive the Power"

We can become buried in life's difficulties if we don't learn how to master our emotions and will. That mastery is never completely realized without God's power working in our behalf by His Spirit. His Word brings us the picture of faith, but it's His power that brings self-control and the rest of the fruit of the Spirit in our life. We need the picture, which is painted for us in the Word of God, but we also need the power to carry it out. That's called grace—the ability of God—working on our behalf. I can have the picture and it will produce faith that it is possible, but the Spirit of God gives me the power to overcome my fleshly appetites and the nagging reminders of my past limitations and insecurities. When we meditate on God's picture, it produces hope and faith in our hearts until the picture on the inside of us matches what God says. You'll *believe* what God says. You'll *expect* what God says. And you'll begin to *see* what God says become a reality in your life. When God's picture is in you, and His power is on you, you can do all things through Christ!

One of the worst things you can die with is wasted potential! Ask yourself, "Am I using my potential? What is holding me back from using my potential?"

The Three Areas That Dictate Our Actions:

Mind: your mental outlook, mindset or belief system

Will: your choices, priorities, and desires

Emotions: your feelings, attitudes, and reactions to circumstances based on your mindset and desires

Many people are sick and weak because their bodies are reflecting what's in their soul realm. Instead of looking to God, people allow themselves to become convinced of their identity outside of God's Word. In James 1:23-24, we see an example of this. He said, "Anyone who listens to the word but does not do what it says is like someone who looks at his face in a mirror and, after looking at himself, goes away and immediately forgets what he looks like." We can find our identity in God, but if we don't continuously renew our minds with the truth, we forget what the mirror of the Word says. We forget who we are and what we're capable of. It's not enough to know what God's promises say; we must choose to let our faith in those promises lead or rule our lives instead of our will or emotions.

We can miss our purpose if we let our feelings direct our actions. When we realize who we are in Christ and what we have in Him, we discover what we can do and how we should do it.

Colossians 1:16 says, "Everything got started in HIM and finds its purpose in HIM." (MSG, author's emphasis)

When we sync up with God, we discover our purpose. We find our part in "His" story! People who make a lasting contribution to history or became world-changers have harnessed their emotions to work for them and not against them. Their purpose became greater than the day-to-day troubles and the emotions, pains of rejection, failure and disappointments that came along the way. They rose to their purpose *coupled* with their emotions to meet the challenge at hand. They learned to let their emotions energize them but not control them. There's a powerful difference.

Mastering the Art of Positivity

The Bible tells us that when we're living life in the Spirit, the fruit of that should be love, joy, peace, patience, kindness, goodness, faithfulness, gentleness and self-control in our lives. Those result in positive emotions! The gifts of the Holy Spirit are gifts to help us demonstrate the power of God, but it's the fruit of the Spirit that demonstrates the love and character of God. They work hand-in-hand as a gift-wrapped package. It's nice to receive a gift, but that gift is even more attractive and beautiful when it's specially wrapped. All too often we want to force others to think or believe what we want, but without presenting ourselves in a positive aspect, whether it's a business proposition or the life-changing gospel, negativity can spoil the possibility of a great outcome. The product can be great, but our "wrapping" may keep others from wanting the package.

Every single attribute of the fruit of the Spirit is positive and essential to our character. Patience and long-suffering can be the holding force to see our vision through until completion. Without it, we can give in quickly to negative circumstances when all we really needed was to have more staying power to fight the good fight to victory. Self-control helps us harness our feelings so that they don't run roughshod over relationships with outbursts of anger and fits of rage or even more subtly but deadly with sharp, critical words. Self-control gives us the power to hold our tongue until a better time to speak with more composure and thoughtfulness. Where there are many words, there is much sin (Proverbs 10:19). If you are a person of many words, ask God to help you use those words in a way to honor and inspire others. When angry, **pray** first and allow the Holy Spirit to help you with the best use of your words. Then find an acceptable way to **process** and break down the situation into some form of **positive action**. Lastly, look for the right **timing** to address the situation.

Pray ➡ **Process** ➡ **Positive action** ➡ **Timing**

Every manifestation of the fruit of the Spirit is the working of love. How do we cultivate love? By cultivating the fruit of love. That's what love looks like. Love is kind – *kindness*. It's patient – *patience*. It displays goodness, faithfulness and self-control. When we allow these to garner and work in our life, they bring *peace* and *joy*, giving our lives true freedom. To be held captive by negative thoughts and actions is to be controlled not by the Spirit, but rather by others and their actions, and oftentimes by oppressive spirits like the spirits working in the women at my speaking invitation.

In contrast to the nine fruit of the Spirit, there are hundreds of emotions we could label "negative." But in a way, emotions are emotions. They really aren't negative, but rather they are neutral in the sense that they are reactions to something we experience. The actions we take determine their negativity or positivity. If I feel fear there is probably some sort of danger or perceived concern. How do I respond to that danger? If it is a real threat that I am responding to, my "feelings" or emotions could give me the indicator I need to react. We must analyze the situation to determine whether there is a real danger or whether we are responding to a perception from pre-programmed experiences or past hurts. Processing the right reaction to the perceived danger determines whether I succeed or not in handling the situation. For instance, I can feel a sense of fear as the roller coaster begins to climb the first and longest hill, anticipating the fast and furious decline. But in the process of evaluating the situation, I analyze the danger along with the fact that the roller coaster is designed to handle the hill safely. Now I can turn my fear into excitement and eventually gratification of tackling that hill. I might even put my hands up next time because I faced the fear and conquered it. On the other hand, if there is a tiger on my back porch and I stumble upon it, my response may be different!

The real key to turning every emotional response or feeling into positive action is analyzing the apparent situation from God's perspective instead of just mine. Regardless of the circumstance, God has a higher perspective of the problem or conflict. I'm not just speaking metaphorically either! He has an answer to the situation and the proper response, and he can lead me and give me the power to act as He guides me through the turmoil.

I am reminded of a situation where an angry mob sought to destroy Jesus but the Bible says that God caused Him to slip through the crowd (John 10). God can give you His ability to walk through a difficult situation by letting Him show you the proper response and even divine strategy, whether it may be a relationship breakdown, a hostile crowd, an empty bank account or a doctor's negative report. God has a positive course of action to get you to your destination.

Emotion Kick-start Challenge:

___ **Find the silver lining.**

> Turn a difficult situation into an adventure. When you encounter a negative, don't focus on it. Look for a redemptive way to handle trouble, setbacks and problems.

___ **Persuade someone to do something using the power of emotions.**

> As an experiment, capitalize on the persuasive potential of our emotions by motivating someone into action using emotions.

___ **Set a personal goal and use an emotionally compelling incentive.**

> Want to eat healthier? More effectively manage your time? Use the end result as a motivator and let your feelings drive you to create new positive habits.

MAKE UP
YOUR MIND

Chapter 2

Our minds play a big part in the course of our hearts and emotions, leading us one direction one minute, only to send us running a different direction the next. Did you know that many, if not most of our emotional responses to situations, are learned and eventually become a habit? This can be a positive skill when we renew our mind with God's Word, but when we feed ourselves the wrong messages, our thoughts can mislead our emotions. Our minds are like the GPS, and our emotions are the destination. Whatever we think on comes out in our attitudes and feelings. I've heard some people say they can't listen to a certain type of music because it makes them feel easily agitated throughout their day. What we think on directs our emotions.

Remember when you were devout about something as a young teen, and your mother told you it was just a phase? In the moment you felt convinced you would never change your mind, but as the years went by, your mother's words proved correctly. Not only are our emotions fickle, but our *opinions* can be fickle as well. And when we attach our emotions to an idea that isn't grounded on God's Word, we are blown around like leaves caught in the wind. So how do we discern emotional *fact* from *fiction?*

Have you ever met a flighty person? I've had acquaintances where every time I spoke to them they talked about their *next* big thing. Whether it was a new man or a new business, they could never stay in one place for long. One week God was telling them to move overseas and care for orphans, and the next week God had "changed" His mind. They took their emotions at face value and allowed their feelings to lead them on a wild goose chase. At the end of the day they had a million beginnings without an end. They had nothing to show for their efforts. Commitment and contentment become impossible when we can't manage our emotions. If we don't understand why we feel the way we feel, we'll always be trying to guess what our heart wants. We chase our emotions around, trying to locate what will finally satisfy us.

Separate Facts from Feelings

When we take a closer look at how our emotions relate to our thoughts, we find that our feelings can be mind over matter. The words "thoughts" and "feelings" are interchangeable, and likewise, it's hard for us to determine what's in our heads versus what's in our hearts.

Our will and emotions start as a small thought—an idea that we tolerate, nurture and slowly accept as a part of us. We cultivate those thoughts until we feel a certain way, or desire a specific thing.

Step 2: *Separate facts from feelings to keep emotions from dictating your destiny.*

Love at first sight is a great example of how our minds can deceive our hearts. Let's say two people have never spoken before, and it's their first time meeting. If the two people make eye contact for a second too long, or if one of them receives a charming smile from the other, it can trick their brains into thinking they're in love. Infatuation is a fickle emotion; it loves the way people make you *feel* instead of loving the person. It imitates love without the foundation for it.

That's when the mind decides to put in its two cents about the meeting. Entertaining a small thought, like, *"I might like this person,"* the mind begins to meditate on only the good qualities that it knows about this person, which at this point are very little. The mind quickly overlooks any negative traits, being so focused on all the benefits of marriage itself. These positive marriage thoughts begin to speak on behalf of this person, *"I think I love this person. Maybe I should marry this person?"* And now, when a conversation is finally sparked, the brain goes into overtime. At this point the girl's perspective of her suitor is blinded by her own desire of marriage and to be loved. Her mind will do everything it can to ignore any facts that threaten her idea of their happiness. You've heard the saying, "Love is blind," right? Well, it's true!

We See What We Want To

Susan is feeling a little lonely when she meets Collin, a charming businessman who makes a great first impression. Susan thinks she has met the one. She doesn't know much about Collin; in fact, they've only just met, but Susan already feels certain she has a future with him. She goes home and thinks about the evening over and over again. Each time, it seems more magical. She's infatuated. Susan thinks she knows the type of man Collin is based on one date.

When Collin asks Susan on a second date, she

agrees. This time Collin is more comfortable with her—they converse and she has a chance to really see him in action. The more they talk, the more red flags there are. Susan sidesteps Collin's shortcomings, convinced his actions are out of character for him. She wants to protect

"The closer we are to a person, the harder it is to make out their character flaws. "

the image of Collin she fell in love with, so she ignores any evidence that threatens that idea. It's not intentional, but merely a common trick our minds play on us. Later in the relationship when Collin does something wrong, it catches Susan completely off guard. *This isn't like Collin,* she thinks. In truth, Susan doesn't *know* what Collin is like. When Susan finally breaks off the relationship, she asks herself, "What did I ever see in that guy?"

The answer? Not much!

Our minds can take what little we know about a person and fill in the gray areas, creating cases for or against them based on what we *want* to see. This can make us feel like we know a person better than we actually do. The longer we know and observe someone, the more clearly we see him or her. Bad first impressions can be rectified, and good first impressions can be confirmed or refuted.

So what's the secret to overcoming this common blunder? *Test* your thoughts before you act on them. The Bible tells us to "take every thought captive." (2 Corinthians 10:5) Separate fact from fiction before your emotions rule your destiny. Recognize that your thoughts can be greatly influenced by your emotions, and if you don't guard your heart *and* your mind, you may be in for an emotional roller coaster.

According to studies, when we love somebody, the parts in our brain that decide whether they are a good person or not shut down. The closer we are to a person, the harder it is to make out their character flaws. Yikes! The most interesting part of the study to me was that the results were the same whether it was romantic love or maternal love.[1] That's why recognizing our children's shortcomings and helping them "right their wrongs" can be the hardest task as parents.

When my firstborn was a baby, I felt like she could do no wrong. Even when she began to test the limits, it was easier to find it funny rather than a serious offense. Those years were the hardest to discipline. However, when

[1] BBC News. "Science proves that love is "blind." http://news.bbc.co.uk/2/hi/health/3804545.stm (accessed August 23, 2016).

I saw someone else's children act in those "funny" ways, I thought, "Hello? Aren't you going to discipline them?" The Bible warned us it's easier to find a speck in our neighbor's eye than a plank in our own (Matthew 7:3-5).

This emotional process can lead us to act before we think, but when it's managed, it's a powerful tool and a *gift* that God gave us. God hardwired us with the ability to love people unconditionally—to have the love of Christ—a skill that we would fail at under any other circumstance. Thanks to what I call the *unconditional love* DNA God put in us, parents, spouses and friends are able to forgive, forget wrongdoings, see the best in others, trust and be patient with each other.

The Bible called it long before any research was done on the subject. 1 Peter 4:8 says, "Most important of all, continue to show deep love for each other, for *love covers a multitude of sins.*" (NLT, author's emphasis)

The Bible urges us to take every thought captive (2 Corinthians 10:5). Whatever we allow our minds to think on sets us on a physical and spiritual course to produce that thought in our lives with the emotions to back it up. We're warned to guard our heart *above all else,* because everything we do flows from it (Proverbs 4:23). That's a tall order. How are we expected to manage our every thought? To love unconditionally, but use wisdom and lead our emotions?

God never asks us to do something that isn't both good for us, and something He has given us the grace to carry out. Philippians 4:6-7 gives us the key. "Don't worry about anything; instead, pray about everything. Tell God what you need, and thank him for all he has done. Then you will experience God's peace, which exceeds anything we can understand. His peace will guard your hearts and minds as you live in Christ Jesus" (NLT). So we don't have to be afraid to be vulnerable, love, trust or *feel*, but we have to approach every situation with prayer, thankfulness and the peace of God. We have to move in God's timing, testing our hearts with accountability, aware that our feelings can quickly change allegiance from God's Will to our own.

Correcting Our Emotional and Mental Habits

There is a law of the Kingdom of God that says, whatever a man (or woman) sows, that will they also reap (Galatians 6:7). This law applies to everything. What we eat, what we think on, what we say. It also has an impact on our emotions and feelings. If I have deficiencies emotionally from what has been sown into my life by others, my environment, upbringing and myself, those deficiencies will show up in my life. And since we have all been raised in an earth-cursed system, we all have deficiencies, wounds and lack from what we've sown and what others have sown into us.

There are many wonderful natural principles we can learn that will help us deal with our weaknesses and deficiencies. But honestly without the power of an encounter with God's Love and Spirit, those changes and natural methods will fall short of bringing us into a state of wholeness and real lasting freedom. We can learn to accept ourselves and be better communicators, we can forgive others by willpower, but nothing can undo what was done to us or what we have done to others without God. The law of sowing and reaping will keep us in a state of perpetual deficiency. Paul even said, "I do not understand what I do. For what I want to do I do not do, but what I hate I do" (Romans 7:15).

I believe in doing everything we can with natural

knowledge and wisdom, but it's not enough by itself! We need the Spirit of God to help us supersede natural laws that have created deficiencies in our soul. We need God's power, His spiritual truth coupled with practical principles. God's supernatural will give us strength and ability to do in the natural what we could not do in ourselves. He gives us the ability to change and to sow a new thought, and use more powerful Kingdom principles than the natural earthly ways we have learned and lived.

I have seen these principles radically change innumerable people's lives over and over, as well as mine. I have witnessed alcoholics, addicts, and the severely depressed walk free when the natural world and doctors told them there was no hope for their pain and they would only be able to "learn to cope." And while learning to operate in natural ways may be a start in the right direction, complete freedom is much greater, and comes only by the supernatural.

All of your thoughts, actions and reactions originate from your belief system—what you believe about yourself, your worth and your future.

YOUR <u>BELIEF SYSTEM</u> ORIGINATES FROM:

YOUR UPBRINGING - "The Past"
- You didn't choose it.
- You cannot change it.

YOUR CHOICES - "Today"
- You can change it by what you **"Think"**
- You can change it by how you **"Act"** and **"React"**

You didn't choose where you were born or how you were raised, and you can't change it. However, you *can* change what you think, how you act, and how you react to life and people today. How are you acting? With confidence and boldness, or fear and intimidation? How are you reacting when people mistreat you? When negative circumstances happen in life? Let God's Spirit give you the self-control to manage your life instead of being controlled by the people and circumstances around you.

We have to learn to manage our thoughts and emotions about the past and future—where we've been and where we're going. How can we do that? By managing TODAY!

Where you are going is much more important than where you've been. The pathway to tomorrow is bright if you are looking forward with God toward the future. Jeremiah 29:11 says, "'For I know the plans I have for you,' declares the Lord, 'plans to prosper you and not to harm you, plans to give you hope and a future.'" If you are looking forward, you'll move forward. Your spirit will see vision and dream dreams. You will start to set goals to get to that dream, and strategies will develop that give you the motivation to act on your dream. You are what you *think*.

Our dreams will not develop into goals and strategies toward accomplishment if we allow emotional baggage from yesterday to distract us or create enough disturbances to discourage us from the decision to act. Facts are clearer but feelings can become the gray area that stops our progress. The soul (mind, will and emotions) all must work together in a positive direction, moving forward for us to have the right mindset, willful decision making and emotional responses to energize where we're going. I must think right, decide I will do it and harness emotions to succeed. Freedom is a beautiful word but it can only be attained when the natural and the supernatural collide in a powerful way!

Emotion Kick-start Challenge:

___ **Make a list of habits and emotional patterns you've inherited from your family line.**

> Take a moment to consider how your family handles offenses, stressful situations, anger, and so on, and see how your reactions line up. How can you change the negative responses going forward?

___ **Observe situations throughout your week where your emotions take you away from the facts.**

> Watch how you handle different situations every day. Do your emotions get away from you? Do you frequently "make a mountain out of a mole hill?"

___ **Introduce yourself to somebody new.**

> Take note of your first impressions, prejudgments, and assumptions about them. Did they prove correct?

___ **Think about a situation where you made an assumption about a person that turned out to be completely wrong.**

> Reflect on a moment when you misjudged somebody because you didn't have all of the facts.

WILLPOWER
TO ACT

Chapter 3

"I don't feel like working today."

"I don't feel like I love my spouse anymore."

"I don't want to be their friend!"

Feelings that rule our lives will also rule our success. We better make sure they are not only based in truth, but also that if we succumb to the feelings we are experiencing, then they are going to cause us to end up where we want to go! I have seen people give in to feelings that they didn't want to work, resulting in their family becoming destitute financially.

There is a powerful connection between vision, desire and feelings. What would it be like to feel inspired to work and to accomplish a triumphant feat that you were proud of? Let yourself imagine or dream a big dream. Vision paints a picture of a desired end. We are admonished to write the vision and make it plain in Habukkuk 2:2. And at the same time, people perish or quit if there is no vision.

Temptations and distractions present themselves constantly and challenge our resolve and goals. It's easy to take the instant path of gratification, but if my vision speaks of something greater, a burning desire will fuel my emotions and the self-control from God's Spirit enables me to do all things through Christ.

Health and weight loss is a great example. If I picture the short term, I may choose to eat the chocolate cake because I see it and it gives me a burning desire to eat it. But if I see a bigger vision and think vacation, swimsuit and healthy lifestyle, my burning desire is now for something beyond the moment. I say, "No cake for me today!" or "Only one bite!" I feel motivated to stay focused on my goal. Whether we realize it or not, almost every decision we make is weighed against our vision.

If we don't feel like working, we probably have lost vision (or perhaps never had one) that the reward is greater than the immediate lure of the alternative— sleep, watching television, gaming or eating. "A little extra sleep, a little more slumber, a little folding of the hands to rest— and poverty will come on you like a thief..." (Proverbs 24:33-34). Thieves steal and take something unlawfully. How is lack of vision and a burning desire stealing the future from a generation of sleepers?

In the area of relationships, I have seen people pull away from church or friendships because they feel hurt or offended by something that happened. Many years of valuable investment and rewards of enjoyable exchanges can be lost because of feelings of offense. Inevitably, if you confront the silence or impenetrable walls, and ask if something is wrong or if they are offended, they almost always say, "No"; but their actions indicate otherwise. The vision to continue in a relationship must dictate our actions rather than a momentary problem. It's pretty short-sighted and emotionally immature to think that we can have a relationship where there is not an occasional offense or misunderstanding. If we have false expectations of relationships, we will be disappointed and our actions can sabotage what could be a meaningful and deeper friendship if we had the emotional security and foresight to stay with the big picture instead of the momentary challenge.

Anchored on Truth

What does our will have to do with living a life of peace, joy and prosperous relationships and finances? Everything!

Who's in control of our lives? And how powerful is our will to get something accomplished? I grew up with the phrase, "Where there's a will, there's a way." And although it's true, we can will to pursue our own will to our own harm! After I committed my life to God, I made the decision I would live by the reformed statement, "Where there's God's Will, there's a way."

Step 3: *Anchor your choices to truth based on God's Word, or emotions will rule your life.*

Those who know me well know that I have willpower. Once we make a decision to do something or believe something, our will gives us the resolve to stay the course and see it through. Many studies have been done about the will and its effects on decisions and even the will to live. The power of your willpower is greater than any other force, which affects your personal desires, decisions and accomplishments. Even if you decide to give your will over to another person, your will was still involved.

There is something very powerful when a person says, "I will do it" vs. "I will try to do it." *Try* gives us an out. It creates a double-minded state that leaves us room for other options or courses of action. But once a person decides, "I WILL," and it is a sincere single-minded focused decision, look out! So it would stand to reason if you want to accomplish something, eliminate all other options. That could be a frightening endeavor, but if there is hesitation, there's not a "mind-made-up" attitude; and by being double minded, there is no willpower yet anyway. Once you reach the place of "I WILL," you can no longer entertain an alternative or distraction if you want to reach the desired end.

Jesus was in the garden of Gethsemane and asked his friends to pray with Him. His friends chose to sleep, but He chose to pray. In a painful challenge of emotions, Jesus made the decision to let go of His will to do what He desired and felt, in order to follow God's plan for His life. In Luke 22:42 Jesus said, "Father, if you are willing,

"God gives us the power or anointing to do the thing we could not do ourselves."

take this cup from me; yet not my will, but yours be done." There literally was an emotional wrestling match so intense that it resulted in Jesus sweating blood! This is a condition that occurs in intense distress and overwhelming emotional pain. He made up his mind and submitted His will to God in Gethsemane. Gethsemane literally means to press and crush. Jesus was pressed mentally and emotionally but decided, "I WILL." After that, there was no vacillating throughout the process. He walked out the decision to carry out God's will because it became *His* will.

When you and I are pressed mentally and emotionally but decide to forfeit our will for the Father's, we take on His will, and we therefore take on His **grace**! God gives us the power or anointing to do the thing we could not do ourselves.

My family's story is one of those stories! We tried in our own method to build a company and financial success. We were consistently met with our own lack both in business acumen and finances. But when we kept getting pressed by life and eventually wanted to give in to failure, it was at that place we asked God to take complete control of our destiny. Honestly we would have told you we were "sold out" prior to that, but there were more days we tried our will than His. But something changed when the pressure became so great we no longer had confidence to trust in ourselves. At the point we let go and gave Him control of our life—business and desires—something drastically changed. "But seek first the Kingdom of God and His righteousness [or right way of life] and all these things will be added to you" (Matthew 6:33 ESV). We were asking God to bless our way of living, but He asked us to give Him our right to "will" over our life. We transferred the deed to Him, and He became the owner. Now lest that scare you, recognize that He created us so He knows what we are best suited to pursue or do. Remember He created us with purpose, so who is better to help us determine that purpose? "I am not my own, I have been bought with a price." "It is not I that lives, but Christ lives in me." (See 1 Cor. 6:19-20 and Gal. 2:20.)

We had managed to build a company that was having a limited amount of success and were starting to gain some financial relief when my husband began to call me from the office in tears and sometimes in anguish. He was struggling with panic attacks and intense pressure. He began to pray and study scriptures for answers and relief. All that he would tell me was, "Pray for me. I don't know what's going on." Weeks like this went on and on, until one night while lying in bed, I gathered enough nerve to ask, "Are you being called to the ministry to pastor?" He said,

"Yes." Then he rolled over and went to sleep! But I didn't! He had been wrestling with a decision to follow God's will; now my wrestling began. Within days and weeks, well-meaning people would tell me that ministers made no money and that it would be terrible the way people would treat us in ministry. Some ministers said, "IF there's anything else you can do, do it!" Not exactly encouraging but on the other hand, it helped me count the cost. We shared our heart with a trusted minister, and he said, "I've seen that call on you for years." Then we sat down with our children and added their thoughts on the direction we had been sensing and preparing for. Our son, Tim, spoke for the children and said, "If God said it, then that's what we are doing."

Interestingly enough, once we made the decision to align our will with His direction for us, our business didn't go away. God began to breathe His Life into it, and it prospered every year in a greater way to this day. So many times we fear giving God the control of our destiny because we don't trust God. We have learned to trust ourselves and no one else. But "God is not a man, that He should lie..." (Numbers 23:19 NASB). God has purpose and promises far greater than our thoughts and has the way to not only meet our needs but also to give us the desires of our heart.

Jesus chose death on a cross to pay the ransom note on our life, and it wasn't an easy cross to carry. But unless a seed is planted in the earth, it can't grow into a plant bringing a harvest. On the third day, God raised Him from the dead and seated Him on His right hand, and made Him the King of kings and Lord of lords. Little did we know that completely surrendering our will to God would give us so much more in so many ways than what we gave. Really, all we had to offer him was us. We were already at the end of ourselves. At the end of our will is Father God, and His will gives us the ability to say, "I WILL!" and to really mean it. Once we do, it will produce results. Whether you're building a ministry, business or family, decide who will have the deed to your life and if you are willing and obedient, you will eat the good and best of the land. You will enjoy the good life...the God Life.

Am I Making the Right Decision? (The "HALT" Test)

We've discussed the power of the will in making decisions, but how do we assure we make right decisions?

The entrance of God's Word brings light to situations guiding our decisions. So why do we make poor decisions when we often know what is right? Paying attention to our physical and emotional state is important to protect ourselves from making serious mistakes.

If we feel anxious, stressed or fearful, we can be certain that the principle of HALT is at work. When we're **H**ungry, **A**ngry, **L**onely, **T**ired, it's not a good time to make important decisions. Learning to recognize these feelings is important to aid us in knowing when we should take an extra measure of caution with ourselves and our relationships. It's best to "halt" before we do or say something we will later regret. Because pain seeks pleasure to console our hurts, learn to pay attention to signs of neglecting physical or emotional needs, which may lead to poor decision-making or wrong and sinful choices.

Hunger can cause a drop in blood sugar, resulting in irritability and even a short fuse. In addition to physical hunger, there is the hunger for love, acceptance and connection to others. When we are angry our ability to rationally process the facts is affected and we overreact. Loneliness may give us the perception that we are unwanted and unloved. Many a bad relationship decision has been made when feelings of disconnectedness and a yearning to be loved are present. Loneliness is not always the state of being alone but can be a result of feeling misunderstood or undervalued. Perhaps tiredness is the greatest challenge we all face in our busy lives and hectic schedules. When we experience any of these factors—hunger, anger, loneliness and tiredness—we say things we don't mean, and we tend to have a pessimistic outlook on life. Faith is weak and fears are magnified. I could add neglecting our spiritual wellness to this list.

We must learn to take stock of our wellness and take care of ourselves spiritually, physically and emotionally. When we don't trust God, our life gets out of balance. We over work and neglect our bodies with poor eating, lack of exercise and rest. Lack of rest and recreation also affects our emotional well-being. After all, a merry heart does good like medicine.

I had been through a very intense quarter with pressures and problems coming from every direction. I kept telling myself things would get better and I would rest eventually. Every time we thought we would take a break, something came up over and over. I knew my husband and I were not taking care of ourselves but I rationalized that we were doing what God wanted us to do for people. Eventually I found myself feeling resentful and short-fused with situations and people that I normally would handle differently. We were at a ministers' meeting when I learned about a fellow minister who had become sick to the point of death from running himself down and traveling overseas. If that wasn't enough of a warning, a respected minister said I keep getting the word *sabbatical* for you. As I analyzed the last 18 months prior, I realized we had turned every trip into ministry or business. I had slipped into rationalizing that we should do something productive every trip. But the problem was that we were still mentally and emotionally engaged in giving out and working, so true rest wasn't happening. One day my daughter said to me, "Mother, you and Dad can't carry the weight of the world." She was right. I wasn't trusting God; I was trusting my works.

When we are pressed, God's grace is sufficient; but we also must heed the Holy Spirit's leadership or we can find ourselves spiritually and emotionally shipwrecked.

Our life and faith are a marathon, not a sprint. Pace yourself in such a way that you are sharp enough to make informed and good decisions by living a quality of life that fosters health, emotional stability and peace. God rested on the seventh day from his labors and we must rest from ours as well. When we choose to work seven days a week and refuse to take vacations and celebrations because we have too much to do, we are really putting our trust in our work and ability. It's a lack of trust in God and based in unbelief. Our security cannot be in ourselves.

People's tendency to develop unhealthy habits and addictions increases when we live in pain and deny our needs of rest and renewal. Jesus had to get away to a quiet place to pray and hear from God. He laughed, rested, cooked and celebrated with his disciples. We were made for connection with God and others, and we must make quality decisions to protect these times if we are to live free, whole and healthy. HALT when you feel hungry, angry, lonely or tired, and get recharged so you can be your best. I've learned not to make financial decisions, large purchases or have serious discussions with people when I need to HALT; and when I neglect to do so, I'm sorry. Stop everything and let your soul be healed. Matthew 11:28-30 says, "Come to me, all of you who are weary and carry heavy burdens, and I will give you rest. Take my yoke upon you. Let me teach you, because I am humble and gentle at heart, and you will find rest for your souls. For my yoke is easy to bear, and the burden I give you is light."

Emotion Kick-start Challenge:

___ **Make a 5-year dream plan.**

> Look ahead as you write your goals, vision, and wants for the next five years. Put it somewhere you can reference it every day.

___ **Schedule a recreational day a week.**

> Plan a day each week for rest, time with God and fun. If you want to take it to the next level, shut off social media and email for the complete 24 hours.

TRAINING
FOR SUCCESS

Chapter 4

The secular world recognizes five key emotions that all others stem from:

JOY

FEAR

DISGUST

SADNESS

ANGER

These are not new discoveries as they are recorded in God's Word, thousands of years earlier. The Bible describes them as joy, a spirit of heaviness (sadness), a critical spirit (disgust), a spirit of fear (fear), and a spirit of rage (anger). The world's concept tends to focus on the soul but misses the spiritual component. We are a spirit, have a soul and live in a body. Did you know that God has a soul too, and we are made in His image? Leviticus 26:11-12 says, "I will make my dwelling among you, and my *soul* shall not abhor you. And I will walk among you and will be your God, and you shall be my people" (ESV, author's emphasis)

We should not neglect our feelings or emotions any more than we would want to neglect our spirit. God made them both and designed them to work in sync. We don't deny our emotions but rather we subject them to spiritual training. We train them to work for us instead of against us. When we recognize there is sadness, we identify the source and apply the healing of God's Love and Word to give us help and courage in the face of sadness. Hebrews 4:12 says, "For the word of God is alive and active. Sharper than any double-edged sword, it penetrates even to dividing soul and spirit, joints and marrow; it judges the thoughts and attitudes of the heart." Emotions are connected so closely to our spirit and body that our central nervous system and organs react to our emotions and every part of our physical body is affected. That's why handling stress and other factors in a negative way eventually will affect our body. Stress and problems are a part of life, but how we handle it impacts others and ourselves.

Jesus was moved with compassion toward people, and he healed their sick. (See Matthew 14:14.) Compassion is an emotion. Jesus was moved by compassion (emotion) to act and change situations in the physical realm by acting on God's Word. He was touched by what he saw on earth and then touched earth with what He saw from heaven. It's interesting that the shortest scripture is, "Jesus wept"

(John 11:35). Jesus wept over Lazarus' death, and many places in the Word of God we see where God felt a jealous zeal for His children. Emotion moved God, and it can move us as well. The scripture teaches us to mourn with those that mourn and rejoice with those that rejoice. We can share emotionally with others, but our action must be based in God's truth to bring eternal results. Jesus healed all that were oppressed by the devil, for God was working with Him. (See Acts 10:38.) God wants to work with us as we encounter emotional situations; we want to let God's Word instruct us, and let the Holy Spirit direct us. This comes by training.

Have you ever worked out physically and woke up the next day with sore muscles? To accomplish the goal of becoming fit you have to work your muscles. It isn't always pleasant to work or discipline our bodies to maintain a regimen of exercise or healthy eating; however, it produces results in our well-being and muscle tone. The same is true spiritually. Training produces strength, and strength gives us greater capacity. God wants us to discipline our flesh—our soul realm with all its appetites and demands— so that we have a greater capacity to live and model God's

Kingdom for others. Just as you can increase your lifting power by usage, you can increase your capacity to excel for God and succeed in life by training. Training requires discipline, but discipline brings greater results!

Becoming sanctified spirit, soul and body won't happen if we resist this process. Hebrews 12:11 (MSG) gives us insight into God's motive for discipline, "My dear child, don't shrug off God's discipline, but don't be crushed by it either. It's the child he loves that he disciplines; the child he embraces, he also corrects. God is educating you; that's why you must never drop out. He's treating you as dear children. This trouble you're in isn't punishment; it's *training*, the normal experience of children... But God is doing what *is* best for us, training us to live God's holy best. At the time, discipline isn't much fun. It always feels like it's going against the grain. Later, of course, it pays off handsomely, for it's the well-trained who find themselves mature in their relationship with God."

Being well-trained pays off handsomely! That's a promise from God's Word. From the time of birth, we have been trained in selfishness—demanding our own way, throwing temper tantrums and manipulating for personal gain. The only way to change our selfish ambitions and lustful appetites is discipline. We can choose discipline by training ourselves to obey God's Word, or God must discipline us for our own sake. We can resist this training and remain spiritual babies, but if we do so, it is to our own harm. It will show up in some form of consistent financial woes, relationship breakdowns, gossip, church-hopping, physical maladies, out-of-control appetites and other results like the list in Galatians 5:19 (MSG): "It is obvious what kind of life develops out of trying to get your own way all the time: repetitive, loveless, cheap sex; a stinking accumulation of mental and emotional garbage; frenzied and joyless grabs for happiness; trinket gods; magic-show religion; paranoid loneliness; cutthroat competition; all-consuming-yet-never-satisfied wants; a brutal temper; an impotence to love or be loved; divided homes and divided lives; small-minded and lopsided pursuits; the vicious habit of depersonalizing everyone into a rival; uncontrolled and uncontrollable addictions; ugly parodies of community. I could go on. This isn't the first time I have warned you, you know. If you use your freedom this way, you will not inherit God's kingdom."

Wow! That's a list! We want to inherit God's Kingdom—all that Jesus purchased for our lives. We may inherit salvation, but there is much more to the Kingdom in this life as well. The scripture speaks of those who are saved by fire—they just make it into heaven, but their life has been a trial of constant sorts from their choices because they are always hearing but never coming to the knowledge of truth. They don't do what they hear. The Bible calls that deception! There's a saying: "If we all did what we knew, we'd be rich, skinny and happy." We laugh, but in reality we could make our lives tremendously different if we refuse to be a hearer only and become a doer of God's truth.

It may seem difficult to live for a season without a new car to avoid debt, and especially when it looks like everyone else is buying. It could seem mundane at times to live the disciplined life of saving instead of spending, keeping your word when it costs you, staying home with your family instead of going out with the guys, working for your living when others rely on the government undeservingly and you're paying the taxes, and the list goes on and on. When we see others make wrong choices, it would be easy to compromise, rationalize and justify making the same choices, but we must heed the warnings of where this leads. It's not any place good.

> *"For the one who sows to his flesh [his sinful capacity, his worldliness, his disgraceful impulses] will reap from the flesh ruin and destruction, but the one who sows to the Spirit will from the Spirit reap eternal life."* (Galatians 6:8 AMP)

Ruin and destruction...not exactly the picture the culture and media paints of credit card offers, one-night stands, or handing over our freedom to an ever-encroaching government in exchange for government handouts.

Many years ago after a major struggle with business, Gary and I made a quality decision that "we will no longer rely on debt." Not try to avoid debt, but will! This decision was tested many times, and there was a lot of pressure to go back on the decision. We had friends, family and even ministers make statements that we had taken this "getting out of debt thing" too far. I understand where they were coming from. At the time we were living in an 1800s farmhouse and driving an older Peugeot with a bent frame. Had we been willing to use debt, we could have appeared more "prosperous" and had more instant gratification. (By the way, that's what creditors want you to choose!) But our overall vision was bigger than a shortcut fix.

For instance, when we were struggling financially in the early years, we had borrowed about $20,000 from Gary's father, partly to pay for a state-to-state move to Ohio. Borrowing was a bad decision for sure as God had to teach us how to prosper and live free from debt. This debt bothered us continually, and we prayed that we could pay him back. One day Gary's dad told us, "Do not worry about paying me back; I will take it out of your inheritance when I die." Wow, we thought that was awesome, and we thanked him for his generosity. But that night the Lord spoke to my husband and said to not take the offer. The Lord reminded him that his father was not a believer and needed to see not only our integrity to pay him back but also the faithfulness of God in helping us prosper.

Not long after that we had an insurance claim pay us about $22,000. We were so excited. It was a lot of money to us at the time, and we had so wanted a new car. The cars we had were old and unreliable. Saturn cars had just come out, and we had been talking about how great it would be to have a new Saturn. Now with the windfall of cash we were planning to purchase our new car—with cash! But as we were planning to head off to the car dealership, the Lord rebuked us and reminded us that we still owed Gary's father $20,000. We were bummed. That would take all of our cash. Nevertheless, we decided to obey the Lord, and we went to Gary's father's home and walked in and sat down. We said to Gary's dad that we were there to pay him back.

He seemed shocked as he knew our financial situation and the hardships we had been through. He said, "Well, that would be $20,000!" "We know," and we pulled out our checkbook. We could see tears welling up in Gary's father's eyes, and he sat there for a minute. "Wait," he said, "part of that money was a gift. Let's just say $10,000, and we will call it even." Joyfully we wrote out the check. The new Saturn we had been looking at cost $11,500 and we still had $12,000 left. We left his father's house and drove straight to the dealership and paid cash for our new car!

Following God's ways pays off and leads to peace compared to living a life of compromise and shortcuts. In the end, you find that there really are no shortcuts even though at times we are tempted to think there may be. We were committed to living a debt-free lifestyle and that meant loving the people who criticized our moderate lifestyle while at the same time denying our flesh the extra creature comforts others were enjoying. It was difficult at times, and as much as our vision inspired us, when we became free it was even more amazing than we dreamed it would be. The rewards of eventually building our paid-off dream home far surpassed having a thirty-year mortgage on a much lesser home. The few years of denying ourselves things to follow what we felt God had convicted us to do, eventually advanced us much further financially than our critics—with spiritual benefits as well.

Obedience may not seem exciting. It may hurt at times. It cost Jesus, and it will cost all those who will choose to live godly in Christ Jesus. But the reward is eternal life and the freedom of the inheritance we have in Christ. In Luke 21, Jesus is addressing the last days, and He shares all of the signs and the turmoil with lawlessness of those days; He ends with this admonition in verse 10: "For if you stand firm, you will win your souls." (TLB)

God's Word will give us the ability to stand firm and

to become established. His desire is that you and I would possess or win our soul over to God's ways and the fruit He produces from a disciplined life. It's not too late to make a quality commitment to let your soul be sanctified—to allow God to radically change your life in such a way that you will no longer be tossed around like an undisciplined child failing and falling into one bad decision after another. Maturity is the goal of our faith—to become more like Christ and to see ourselves become a living model of God's Word.

In the synagogue and by his parents Jesus was trained, and when the time came, He took the next step and acted on his training. He didn't just hear the Word, He modeled it—He did it—by dying on the cross. And because of His obedience, He was highly exalted by God, seated at His right hand in heaven. When tempted to take our own way of instant satisfaction over God's sanctification, we should remember His example and do the difficult thing instead of the easy way out. Obedience will bring life.

Excuses will hold us in patterns of defeat, always hearing but never coming to the knowledge of the truth. How do we come into the knowledge of truth? By doing what we hear! Acting immediately to begin implementing the changes is necessary to mirror what God's Word says. As we apply knowledge, we get wisdom. Wise people have heard, applied and become wiser with action. Too many people sit on the sidelines of life because they hear and do nothing with it or stop doing what they've heard when they run into difficulty or discouragement. When you see the prize—the vision—keep your eyes focused on it, and do what it takes in the short term to reach the long-term goal.

"Keep your eyes on *Jesus*, who both began and finished this race we're in. Study how he did it. Because he never lost sight of where he was headed—that exhilarating finish in and with God—he could put up with anything along the way: Cross, shame, whatever. And now he's *there*, in the place of honor, right alongside God. When you find yourselves flagging in your faith, go over that story again, item by item, that long litany of hostility he plowed through. *That* will shoot adrenaline into your souls!" (Hebrews 12:2 MSG)

Emotion Kick-start Challenge:

___ **Circle the two emotions that have the greatest impact on your life:**

>   Joy
>
>   Fear
>
>   Disgust
>
>   Sadness
>
>   Anger

___ **Do something daily that will benefit your spirit, soul and body.**

>   Aim to do an activity that improves each area of your life every day. For example, spending time in prayer would edify your spirit, spending quality time with loved ones would edify your soul, and eating a healthy diet would edify your body.

SHORT FUSE

Chapter 5

Gary and I have had our fair share of airport horror stories, but none beat a particular flight from Dallas, Texas, to Columbus, Ohio. We had attended a ministry conference all week and were flying back to get Pastor home in time to preach the weekend services at our church. I am notorious in my family for pushing it to the last second when we're trying to make a flight, but in my defense, we have rarely actually missed any. This day it wasn't my fault we were running late. A friend of ours recommended what time we should leave for the airport, but we forgot to account for returning our rental car. As traffic picked up on the freeway, I knew we weren't making good time.

"I'll drop you off at the gate and return the rental car," I told Gary. "If I make it back in time for the flight, that's great, but if I don't, at least you'll be back to preach the weekend."

Gary was hesitant, but eventually agreed.

We pulled up to our gate where an older man came moseying out to check our bags. We threw our bags out as fast as we could, meanwhile the man was moving slower than molasses. I asked him, "Do you think I'll be able to make it in time?"

"Oh, sure you can," he said.

"That's what I always say!" I thought.

I jumped in the car and told Gary, "I love you, and hopefully I'll see you on the flight. Just look for me."

I sped off as close to the legal limit as I could, every ounce of southern blood in me kicking in. I'm a fighter—I never give up without trying everything I can. The rental car facility was farther than I anticipated, and my cell phone died along the way. Now I had no way to contact Gary.

I pulled up to the ticket machine that guards the entrance to the rental car parking area, and as I rolled down my window to put my ticket in the machine, a gust of wind blew through the car. My parking ticket blew out the window! I yelled out, "In Jesus' name, stop!" I went to open my door to get the ticket, but my door whacked into the little post there. I pulled the car forward as much as I could and squeezed between the door and the post. I grabbed my ticket, climbed back into the car, and stuck it into the machine.

I told myself, "I can do this! I'm going to make it!"

As soon as I got through the gate, I darted to a spot

and parked the car. I pulled out my computer and plugged in my phone to charge it. I climbed out of the car and told the lady working there, "I'm in a really big hurry."

"Okay," she said, "I'll go to the other side." She opened the car door, and another gust of wind came through the car and blew my boarding pass out. It was gone. It blew over a building.

"Oops! Sorry," she said.

I wanted to get angry, but I directed my anger toward pushing me to move faster and try harder to catch my plane.

When I went to grab my bag in the back seat, it was flipped over. Everything in it was dumped into the floorboard. I started grabbing things as quickly as I could and throwing them back into the tote bag. I left the rental car area, my opened laptop charging my phone in one hand, and my over-stuffed bag in the other. Now I was going to have to get another boarding pass printed, and that was going to take up more time. Time I didn't have.

I needed to catch a shuttle bus to get to the airport terminal. I passed a sign that said buses C and D were left, and E and F were right. I turned left and climbed on the bus, still hopeful that I would make it despite so many setbacks. Several other people were on the bus, and we were all going to terminal C. The bus stopped, and the driver announced, "Terminal *D*."

"You're going to C next, right?" I asked.

"No," he said. "We go all the way around the whole airport to terminals E and F before we get to C."

Inside I told myself, *"Joy. I've got joy. Don't lose your joy, Drenda."*

I didn't get angry, but one of the other passengers did. As a good Christian woman, I should have encouraged him to keep his peace, but as a woman who was running late for her flight, I was inwardly shouting, *"Go you!"* Don't you love when someone says what you're thinking? We pleaded with the man to take us to terminal C (since we were all going there anyway), but he refused. We would have to switch buses. The whole bus—annoyed and running late for different flights—emptied, and everyone got in line for the next bus.

As soon as we arrived to terminal C, I took off for the guest services kiosk and asked the lady to print me off a new boarding pass.

"It's too late to check in," she said.

"I'm already checked in," I said quickly. "I just need you to reprint my boarding pass because it blew away."

"Oh, you'll have to go up to the counter," she said.

Joy.

I ran up to the counter and asked them to print me off a new boarding pass.

"Here it is," the worker said. "But you won't make it."

I sprinted to the TSA security line and frantically threw my stuff into the bins. I was loaded down with things—I had my computer that was charging my phone, I had Gary's coat that he left in the car, my purse, my huge carry-on, and I was wearing heels because we came straight from a conference. I threw it all left and right into bins.

I have TSA pre-check, which usually makes the process quick. Gary and I travel a lot, so I know what I can and can't bring through security. I carry the same cosmetics every time I travel so I know I won't have any issues. I had a perfume bottle in my makeup bag, the same perfume bottle I have flown with hundreds of times, and *this* time it caused an issue.

"Bag check."

I was half-tempted to say, "Keep it all! Just let me go through!"

I could see the gate on the other side of security, but I couldn't see Gary. I tried to text him and let him know I was almost there so he could have them hold open the gate, but one of the guards shouted, "You can't use your phone here!" Of course, I forgot you couldn't use your phone in TSA. They patted me down and searched through my bag.

"Circumstances come that tempt us to lose our joy, but ultimately, how we react to our circumstances is our decision."

Meanwhile, I kept my joy. As soon as they told me I was clear, I took off in a full sprint to my gate. I got there moments after they shut the door, but the plane still hadn't moved. So, being the tenacious person I am, I walked up to the door and started pushing the buttons! (That sounds like a great idea, right?) I pushed "0" hoping it would call an operator. I texted Gary and told him I was right outside the door, but he replied that the flight attendants already gave my seat away. Gary waited by the gate as long as he could try to stall them, but eventually they couldn't wait any longer.

I sat down in half-defeat and waited for one of the workers to come up the ramp. A woman came out and I explained how I had barely missed the flight because I had to drop the rental car off. She said, "Well, if we would have known you were dropping off your rental car, we wouldn't have given your ticket away."

For lack of nicer words, I simply said, "Oh, okay."

I remained by her counter as she began to type. I figured she was rerouting me to another flight since she didn't say anything else to me, so I waited patiently. And I kept waiting patiently. And I waited more patiently. Eventually I asked, "Are you able to check and see if there is another flight I can get on?"

"I can help you with that," she said.

I repeated to myself, *"I have joy, I have joy, I have joy."*

In the end, I was able to fly home a few hours later, and Gary and I both made it home for the weekend services. I was so thankful I didn't step out of God's favor by letting anger take over my emotions. When it was all said and done, things that felt very *big* in the moment turned out to be very *insignificant* in the long run. Circumstances come that tempt us to lose our joy, but ultimately, how we react to our circumstances is our decision.

The enemy would love to get you bitter, negative and critical. He wants you to feel like there's nothing you can do, and you're helpless. We have to renew our minds with what God says so we don't become cynical. We have to run our emotions past the Word of God and ask ourselves: Is it a righteous anger? Is there positive action we can take? Devotion will change your emotion. If you change your devotion, it will give you grace over negative emotions. When we put our trust in God, we have the strength to walk in peace and joy no matter *what* circumstances we're facing. The Bible calls it the peace that "surpasses all understanding" (Philippians 4:7). In other words, you can have peace even when anger, fear or worry could be justified.

Anger can lead us to step out of God's will if we don't manage it, but it can also be a powerful tool that we can use against the devil when we bring it under God's authority.

Recognizing the Issue

Many times our anger comes down to something deeper in us—a hidden emotion, insecurity or hurt. When somebody's words hit that sore spot, it causes us to lose our temper. We may cover that insecurity by justifying our anger with the other person's actions, but the Bible warns us that our hearts can be deceiving, and it's possible that we may not even recognize our true motives. Jeremiah 17:9 says, "The human heart is the most deceitful of all things, and desperately wicked. Who really knows how bad it is?" (NLT)

Our emotions are like onions, with multiple layers of feelings concealing the center, core sentiment. Rarely are we angry for anger sake. We might have anger on the surface, insecurity below it, and the fear that nobody loves us at the core. If we dig deeper we find the origin—a second emotion, insecurity or memory that sets us off. When we evaluate ourselves in a greater way, we can learn more about the root of the emotions that drive us.

Step 4: *Anger is a secondary response or emotion.*

Identify why you are angry and deal with the root emotion, then you can focus toward fixing the problem instead of being angry without resolve.

Angry on Purpose

When Gary and I were financially struggling, I began to see the traps set to lead people into debt, to get a hold in their marriages, families and homes. It made me angry because I realized this wasn't just something we fell into, but this was an elaborate plan to consume people with financial bondage. I saw how my family had been hurt because of the traps laid out by bankers, mortgage companies and marketing operations. It was our choice to buy into them, but we weren't the only people making those wrong decisions—there was a clear path people were hopping on that seemed to lead to a good life, but only led to desolation. So when we were going through those financial hardships, I vowed to God, "If you help us get out of debt, and you show us how to live life, succeed in marriage and raise our children, I will spend my life helping others do the same."

Our culture spends a lot of time training us on frivolous things but not on how to raise our families, manage our finances or maintain our marriages. Those three topics are at the foundation of everything we do, everything we are, and yet nobody teaches about it in school. That made me angry, and I knew Gary and I had to do something about it. We needed to teach people God's truth about the most practical areas in their life.

Anger inspires action. Anger drives us to act on our beliefs, whether it's for a positive or negative cause. If somebody is wronging our family, a righteous anger inspires us to protect them. Paul told us to be angry but do no sin (Ephesians 4:26). Sex trafficking *should* make us angry! The slaughter of unborn babies *should* make us angry! Removing God's standard from government *should* make us angry! If we believe what God says, these things should make us want to stand for what's right.

Anger is not a sin itself, but when it is directed at a person, it can lead us to act in a sinful way. And if we don't guard our hearts, anger can become hatred, bitterness or malice. Unrighteousness should anger us and inspire us toward positive action. Psalm 97:10 says, "Let those who love the LORD *hate* evil, for He guards the lives of His faithful ones and delivers them from the hand of the wicked." (author's emphasis)

If I stay angry and don't direct it toward positive action, I'm going to become bitter or act negatively. Anger is only healthy if it drives us to take action that promotes God's truth. Jesus showed us the kind of righteous anger we should have in Matthew 21. Jesus was going to the temple to teach, but when He arrived, He found merchant tables set up by sellers who were looking to profit off of the people earnestly seeking God. In verse 12 it says that Jesus, "entered the temple courts and drove out all who were buying and selling there. He overturned the tables of the money changers and the benches of those selling doves. 'It is written,' He said to them, 'My house will be called a house of prayer,' but you are making it 'a den of robbers'" (Matthew 21:13). How many Christians allow a "den of robbers" to remain in their homes because they are too passive to act?

Religion is the number one thing that we saw Jesus getting angry about in the Word of God. He got angry when the Pharisees criticized people and looked down their noses at them. He didn't like when people judged others instead of loving and helping them. God has not called us as believers, as people who say we love Jesus, to be critical and judgmental of others. Luke 11:46 says, "Jesus replied, 'And you experts in the law, woe to you, because you load people down with burdens they can hardly carry, and you yourselves will not lift one finger to help them.'"

Often the things that make us the angriest can point us toward our destiny. Usually there is one thing that we are more passionate about than another, and when we identify that, it can give us a key to what drives us. For me, I have always been enthusiastic about helping people fulfill their destiny.

One evening a friend and I were sorting through my cabinets. She pulled out a stack of lotion bottles with hardly a squirt left in them, and asked, "Are these trash?"

"No!" I exclaimed. "Those are still good."

She laughed and said that was just like me—I wanted everything to fulfill its purpose, down to the last drop of my lotion bottles. And it's true. When I see people in bad situations, stifled from their futures by the lies of the enemy, a mama bear comes out in me. I want to do everything I can to help.

So what makes you passionate? What makes you angry? How can you direct that anger into positive action?

We can't be passive about spreading God's Kingdom and truth. I don't understand when Christians separate themselves from politics. Every ounce of freedom we have comes down to government. If it's not the Christian's job to vote, whose is it? Should we let people who don't believe in the law of God create the laws that govern us? Edmund Burke put it best when he said, "The only thing necessary for the triumph of evil is for good men to do nothing." We have to be angry about the right things, and act in accordance with the Word of God.

Emotion Kick-start Challenge:

___ **Examine areas that consistently make you angry or passionate.**

> Find your passion points and routine causes of anger. Diagnose if it's something you can turn into positive action, or if it's an area you need to improve in or change altogether. If your morning drive leaves you irritated, map out an alternative route. Create solutions for situations that frequently make you mad.

___ **Take up a form of exercise.**

> Go on a run, do a cardio routine, or learn a physically active hobby. Exercising 3-5 times a week helps release unresolved emotions and creates a more stress-free life.

___ **Take up a cause and do something about it.**

> If something makes you mad, do something useful about it and be the change. Join a committee, show your support at a political convention, or inspire a positive difference at your child's school. We feel happier when we are empowered to act.

DREAD NO MORE

Chapter 6

The wealthiest businessperson, the most attractive celebrity, the talented leader or the faithful minister all face fear. Fear does not discriminate regardless of any factor in life. Those with great success have just learned to conquer many of their fears—to rise above defeat and debilitating feelings of fear. People can fear not having money or losing the money they have. They can fear a disease or losing health. They can fear rejection or failure. And when fear enters into a situation, it begins to take control because fear is not an emotion, it is a spirit.

God has not given you a spirit of fear...
(2 Timothy 1:7)

Fearful emotions are learned reactions. The ones that can handicap us the most are tied to extremely strong emotions. The aftermath of how we think and manage memories of trauma is more important than the actual event. In the circumstance, we may rise to the occasion and do what is needed, but how do we process it afterward? What thoughts do we allow to ruminate in our minds, and what emotionally charged vows do we make once we have come through them?

I have faced many fears in life. When my husband and I were first married, we had great aspirations for success in business that we would use as a platform for ministry. Naively, we expected it to happen too quickly. Our dreams and goals were solid, but our strategy, knowledge and character still needed development. Financial pressure tried to drown our dreams in a mountain of debt. We made emotional decisions to use credit cards for things we couldn't afford; some were needs and others were occasional splurges to soothe our self-pity.

Feelings of failure challenged our dreams. Many times we were on the brink of quitting to get a "good job" instead of pursuing our dreams of freedom and finances by owning a successful business. Those hardships actually worked for us. By facing the challenges of debt, we were inspired to alter the purpose of our business from simple financial services to passionately helping people get out of debt. Later, we added a stronger focus on helping people invest solidly and safely. Each problem or setback we personally encountered gave us inspiration and courage to forge new concepts in business. Our hardship could have been the destruction of our business had we allowed negative feelings and emotions to stop us, but our gained victory and knowledge propelled us further into our destiny.

I can honestly say that every opportunity in my life was met with fear that I had to overcome. Whether it was entering marriage, parenting, business, public speaking or writing, I faced fear. Sometimes I gave in to it for a season, but not for long because God had placed a vision in me that continued to stir my heart. Instead of giving in to fear, it became a passionate fight to not only win for myself but to help others win too. Admittedly I often felt crippled by fear and pressures, but God's Word gave me the ability to fight fear of failure and advance. Challenging fear and standing up to it will change you and your destiny as well.

If you will face your fear, you can help others face theirs!

Step 5: *Turn the negatives into fuel to fight harder.*

Mindsets Based in the Past

Every time we encounter a hardship or hurt in life,

our human response is to store the memories, feelings and emotions of that hurt and create a belief system about those situations. In almost every decision, we consult our existing belief system. If we believe the same experience will happen in the next attempt, we are programmed to stay in that mindset and actually create the same results. This can work for us if we have positive reinforcement, but if our experiences are negative or incite fear, we are set up for failure or we will retreat like a self-fulfilling prophecy.

Often we build a wall of defense after hurtful experiences in order to protect ourselves from future similar encounters and to insulate ourselves from being hurt again. Our conclusions can be irrational and extreme or cause us to re-enter similar situations with expectations they will reoccur, and they almost always do when we believe so. Then wrong beliefs get a stronghold on our belief system. This is why it is imperative we renew our minds to God's Word and receive healing for our emotions. Allowing ourselves to feel better is part of this healing. Just because someone or something has hurt us in an area doesn't mean we should close ourselves off from attempting to do what God says we can do or have what He says we have in Christ Jesus.

Particularly in the area of love this is true. Often when someone has been through a painful marriage, they harden their heart and wall-off their heart, believing that they could never experience joy in a long-lasting relationship. The enemy is all too quick to oblige their pain by substituting counterfeit plans or pursuits. Unresolved hurt can turn into fear and paralyze people from being able to move forward. The answer to this is to renew the mind to what God says about the situation, forgive yourself and others who have inflicted wounds or made poor decisions. Everyone makes mistakes and the only perfect example is Jesus.

Analyze what went wrong, letting the Word of God be your guidepost, and separate your belief system from the actual event. Just because your marriage was painful doesn't mean all marriages must be painful, and therefore marriage is to be avoided at all costs. To believe all marriages will be dysfunctional would be adopting a wrong belief system based on feelings not facts. That is not scriptural or rational. Just because you encountered bankruptcy doesn't mean that you are doomed to repeat it again. Just because slavery existed in the past, doesn't mean that every person of a different race is a bigot and out to take advantage of other ethnicities. Just because a family member died of a certain disease doesn't mean you will.

Irrational fears and painful memories can hold us captive in a prison of "defeat and repeat" and cause us to disconnect from the possibility of a great future.

Prepare to Fight

No matter what we endeavor, whether it is love or financial success, both come with challenges and require a price. When difficulties arise, if you haven't made up your mind and will that you can do all things through Christ, trials and self-defeating feelings will kick in; quitting is the natural response, but rarely the best one. Any worthwhile endeavor will take an all-out commitment and a fight for the promises of God's Word. Spiritual warfare is a reality, and we can sell ourselves short thinking that success will come easily without a fight.

Too often people assume if God is in something, it will be effortless. On the contrary, we have an adversarial force trying to stop us from following God's plan. If our mental and emotional responses agree with the problem instead of with God's Word, we will not have the force to create answers to combat the problem. We must be convinced that there is an answer and we can win. Pressure seems to consistently be at its greatest before a breakthrough, like drilling through a hard surface. The heat intensifies in the thick of it. The saying, "It's always darkest before the dawn" definitely has merit.

We can develop peace and joy in the storms, but there are thunderclouds we encounter in all endeavors to build our lives. I say, develop peace and joy because our initial and natural response is NOT peace or joy in a storm. We have to train our senses how to respond in a storm. We do not naturally sleep in a boat during a storm, remaining calm and responding from our spirit instead of from our emotions. Panic and fear are our typical defaults. We must develop and grow spiritual muscle by exercise to respond differently. When we respond with faith in God's Word, storms must calm and mountains must move. Not only do you have natural senses, you have spiritual senses too. Both must be exercised to discern the best direction. Allowing your spiritual senses to be exercised will help you make right decisions and handle stronger more rewarding challenges. This comes with experience.

> *"But strong meat belongs to them that are of full age, even those who by reason of use have their senses exercised to discern both good and evil."* (Hebrews 5:14, American KJV)

TRAUMA/HURT + WRONG BELIEFS

DEFEAT AND REPEAT

REWIND + CORRECT BELIEFS

WHOLENESS AND BOLDNESS

Eyes Fixed on Freedom

Anytime you or I face difficulties in life, we must rewind and examine and challenge our experience against the Word of God, and let it shine light on the situation. It's easy to succumb to feelings of defeat or trauma, but we are called to surrender only to God's plan. Correcting our thought patterns and belief system to His Word positions us to receive wholeness, healing and the boldness to move forward with life. This is not disregarding what has happened or denying the facts; it's recognizing there are higher laws than our experiences. Although we can't make people's choices or change some factors, we can decide what we will believe and choose. The Word of God gives us the confidence and knowledge to become whole and embark on its picture of us with boldness in faith.

In the last days, scripture says, "Men's hearts [will fail] them for fear..." (Luke 21:26 KJV). As lawlessness increases, people will find it more difficult to discern between what is right and wrong, and their fear will result in irrational beliefs and corresponding actions that will literally bring death. As we see destruction reported in the news and hear fearful messages all around us, we must remember to keep our gaze steadfastly fixed on Jesus, and let the Word of God champion our lives. Psalm 91 (NLT) must be our stand:

"Those who live in the shelter of the Most High

will find rest in the shadow of the Almighty.

This I declare about the Lord:

He alone is my refuge, my place of safety;

he is my God, and I trust him.

For he will rescue you from every trap

and protect you from deadly disease.

He will cover you with his feathers.

He will shelter you with his wings.

His faithful promises are your armor and protection.

Do not be afraid of the terrors of the night,

nor the arrow that flies in the day.

Do not dread the disease that stalks in darkness,

nor the disaster that strikes at midday.

Though a thousand fall at your side,

though ten thousand are dying around you,

these evils will not touch you.

Just open your eyes,

and see how the wicked are punished.

If you make the Lord your refuge,

if you make the Most High your shelter,

no evil will conquer you;

no plague will come near your home.

For he will order his angels

to protect you wherever you go.

They will hold you up with their hands

so you won't even hurt your foot on a stone.

You will trample upon lions and cobras;

you will crush fierce lions and serpents under your feet!

The Lord says, "I will rescue those who love me.

I will protect those who trust in my name.

When they call on me, I will answer;

I will be with them in trouble.

I will rescue and honor them.

I will reward them with a long life

and give them my salvation."

There is a refuge from fear when we come under the protection of the Most High. When trouble comes, we can be assured that we are not facing it alone and can triumph with God's rescue plan resulting in long life. Psalm 91:4 (NLT) says, "...His faithful promises are your armor and protection." Trusting God's love and care for us brings peace and a confident courage to engage life and possibilities when dread would try to hold us back.

Dread and worry are responses to fear. In Psalm 91:5, we are instructed not to dread. Dread plays on past difficulties and painful memories, turning them into future crippling forces. Worry frets about tomorrow, while dread chains us to the past. We need to recognize this spirit operating to immobilize us and to remove the joy of accepting opportunities and responsibilities. Dread is often rooted in insecurity and the fear of failure.

Many years ago, God began to deal with me about starting women's ministry and conferences, but I was hesitant and felt extremely inadequate. I had spent many years as a youth leader, but to face the inevitable insecurities of working with women frightened me. I made it through the first women's conference while facing personal fear, praying fervently and engaging my desire to help women—more than my anguish. My "yes" became bigger than my fear. It was a wonderful relief once it successfully ended. Then I felt the Holy Spirit nudge me, "This is not the last but the first of many." I felt dread begin to creep into my thinking. Strangely I had no reason to dread since I thoroughly enjoyed the conference, but now dread was robbing me of the experience and the future. The more I let it go unchecked, the more it grew. I began to think of ways to get out of it or turn it over to someone more qualified, but I knew God was not going to let me hide. It became a nagging feeling and I was miserable. Incapacitated, I procrastinated what I should do. Miserable, I had allowed myself to entertain dread-filled thoughts and feelings. Eventually I worked through these and continued to move forward, but not without a fight against feelings.

Is Dread Stealing Your Joy?

How might you be inviting or entertaining dread in your life? It can be subtle, more so than other forms of fear. Honestly, dread accounts for numerous stolen destinies and the failure to launch. How are feelings ruling your life over Christ and His plans for you? Instead of rehearsing the anxiety over the conference, I should have managed my memories—focusing on the great outcomes, allowing myself to celebrate the victory and rehearse the joy of changed lives instead of the price or my insecurity. I had to confess my sin of dread as unbelief because I chose to believe that the negative outweighed the blessing God promised me. When the Holy Spirit unveils the root of our fear, it is always some form of unbelief (wrong belief) holding us hostage. Confessing it to God and turning from our false belief to a confident expectation of His promise changes everything.

Recognize it is a normal human response to face dread when you attempt projects or accomplishments outside of your comfort zone. What you do when dread rears its ugly head determines the outcome. Instead of agonizing over just getting through something, make yourself embrace the challenge and attack it sooner than later. Accept that you are given the opportunity because you have potential and something to offer. It's important to recognize that you will not have a perfect outcome every time. So what? That has happened to everyone.

Living Out of Your Comfort Zone:

1. Face the challenge head-on.

2. Allow yourself freedom to make a few mistakes.

3. Let go of false expectations of perfection.

4. Refuse to engage in destructive self-talk.

5. Rehearse how much better you will get at it each time you repeat the challenge.

6. Look for opportunities to do it again quickly so you don't have too much time to build a roadblock to future successes.

Perfection is impossible, so change your expectation to doing your best. If you give each opportunity your personal best, you're on the road to success. Get better, not bitter, when things go wrong as they sometimes will, and refuse to beat yourself up if you miss the mark or have a bad performance. There is no road to success without some setbacks; just don't quit! Success in any endeavor is built one block at a time, so start with the first step. You don't have to be perfect to be amazing.

Shutting Down Fear in Every Form

Fear can take many forms—anxiety, stress, worry, dread and intimidation, to name a few! How do we combat bad news and fearful messages of war, rumors of war, disease, radical extremism and evil? We put on the armor of God covered in Psalm 91 and Ephesians 6. God's armor protects us, reassuring if God is with us, we can have confidence in the face of fear:

Read Ephesians 6:10-17 (NLT) as you stand in

confidence: "A final word: Be strong in the Lord and in his mighty power. Put on all of God's armor so that you will be able to stand firm against all strategies of the devil. For we are not fighting against flesh-and-blood enemies, but against evil rulers and authorities of the unseen world, against mighty powers in this dark world, and against evil spirits in the heavenly places.

Therefore, put on every piece of God's armor so you will be able to resist the enemy in the time of evil. *Then after the battle you will still be standing firm.* Stand your ground, putting on the belt of *truth* and the body armor of *God's righteousness.* For shoes, put on the *peace* that comes from the Good News so that you will be fully prepared. In addition to all of these, hold up the shield of *faith* to stop the fiery arrows of the devil. Put on *salvation* as your helmet, and take the sword of the Spirit, which is the *word of God.*

Pray in the Spirit at all times and on every occasion. Stay alert and be persistent in your prayers for all believers everywhere" (author's emphasis added).

Is Intimidation Holding You Back?

Intimidation on the other hand is another response associated with fear. We become intimidated when we acknowledge and place more emphasis on the fear of man than on the honor of God. God is fully aware that those who do evil often bully the sincere and just. For every good in this world there are evil forces that wish to hinder and intimidate faithful men and women from their mission. Those who oppose good will boldly, blatantly attack with aggressive behavior if left unrestrained. Honest people hesitate to confront evil because they simply want to mind their own business and live peaceably, yet there can be no peace if we do not confront the aggression of unjust acts and behavior, especially against the innocent.

When Gary and I launched our business in a new location and with a great passion to help people get out of debt, we offered to produce a complimentary plan for debt elimination to clients. Consistently, we ran into people's skepticism and fear that we would charge them even though the complimentary plan was sincerely offered from our burning desire to help people. We didn't understand why it was hard to convince them of our motive. Later we learned the reason for their apprehension...a dishonest businessman had advertised on the same radio station for many years that he would help get people out of debt, but when they met with him, he charged their credit card an exorbitant amount, putting them into greater financial peril. People's fears were unwarranted, but sadly their experience told them differently; and some of them resolved to never get help again.

After a year in business, we were at a business fair teaching financial workshops. Gary had left me in charge of our table for a brief time when the infamous man responsible for the debt sham came to our business booth. With a raised voice, red-faced and veins popping from his brow, he stuck his finger in my face and yelled, "You will go out of business doing this plan for free! There's no way you will make it! You'll go bankrupt!" Even though he was greatly intimidating, I mustered the courage to confront him with what God told us to do to help people and not charge for the plan. He stormed away mad as a hornet. We were cutting into his game, and he was not happy! He eventually went out of business with lawsuits. His schemes and poor business practices made our business tougher initially, but eventually word got out that we were the real deal and delivered what was promised. We have produced tens of thousands of those plans to this day! We were able to build a solid, highly successful life and business helping people, in spite of intimidation and you can too. Don't let anyone intimidate you by their angry voices, attitudes or threats and control.

I am reminded of what Psalm 37 says, "Do not fret because of those who are evil... Trust in the Lord and do good. Then you will live safely in the land and prosper. Take delight in the Lord, and he will give you your heart's desires."

Delight in God and do not fear. Even though we were born into the world's earth-cursed system, Jesus faced the fear of death and overcame. He purchased your **_"God has given us the spirit of faith, and it conquers the spirit of fear every time."_** freedom over fear. Master God's Word and wield it like a sword to defeat demonic forces of fear. Second Timothy 1:7 says that God has not given us a spirit of fear but of love and of power and a sound mind. I like to break it down this way: Because I am _loved,_ I have _power_ from the Holy

Spirit over fear; I think right thoughts from a *sound mind,* eliminating fear. If we honestly believe that God loves us and wouldn't do anything to harm us, and He's actually made solid promises to you and me, what is there to fear? The Bible calls them precious promises that include everything that pertains to life and godliness. Yet, fear unaddressed and unchallenged is the greatest stronghold, and the fear of death is the greatest opposition. Jesus conquered death and fear of all forms, and you possess the same victory when you identify with Him instead of yesterday's hurt and trauma.

It's time to challenge any mental or emotional strongholds that may be imprisoning you from complete freedom in Christ. Take an inventory of your life. What fearful feelings are ruling you from pursuit of your dreams? What is the first step toward your destination? The next step? What can you do today that you have been procrastinating? It's time to take back your life.

Because fear is not an emotion, but rather a spirit undergirded by pain and hurt, you must speak to it as you would a robber breaking into your home. You must command it to leave and not give any opportunity for

it to further control you. Jesus said, "I have given you...
authority over all the power of the [evil one] and nothing
by any means shall harm you." (See Luke 10:19.) You have
power over the spirit of fear, so enforce your victory. This
victory is not based on feelings, so once you make the stand
against fear, no longer consult your feelings and instead
stand on your faith. God has given us the spirit of faith,
and it conquers the spirit of fear every time.

Make this declaration:

Father, I thank You that You have not given me a
spirit of fear. I am loved, and perfected love casts out fear.
I have power over fear, and I have the power by Your Spirit
to think sound thoughts. I come under Your protection and
submit myself to You. I resist the enemy and he has to flee.

In the Name of Jesus, I demand the spirit of fear to
leave me! All dread, worry, anxiety, intimidation and every
form of fear must submit to Jesus Christ. Fear, go from me
now! I refuse every thought or feeling that would try to take
me captive. I am free in Jesus' Name. Fear has no authority
over my life because I belong to God. I think His thoughts;
I have His protection, and I can do what He says I can do!

Emotion Kick-start Challenge:

__ **Talk about your fears with a godly friend or mentor.**

> Talking about your fears in a positive environment can be a form of facing them—and nearly as fulfilling!

__ **Do something that's out of your comfort zone daily.**

> The more you are acquainted with the feeling of overcoming fear (even with small things), the easier it becomes. Practice allowing your adrenaline to drive you forward instead of hold you back.

__ **Journal your victories.**

> Every time you successfully face your fears, write about it. Brag on yourself, how you felt afterwards and the role God had in the situation. Keep the journal somewhere you can easily access for encouragement when you have to face something that provokes fear.

HAPPINESS STARTS HERE

Chapter 7

There's an old saying, "When we don't feel so good, we don't do so good." Our feelings can paint a dismal picture of our potential and future success. When we feel discouraged, inadequate, rejected, unloved or undervalued, our performance and ability to communicate love are impacted, reinforcing negative feelings. We spiral into a cycle of defeat and repeat. Change is required to stop the downward fall—a change of scenery or a change of environment can help—but a change in the way we think and how we respond emotionally are the greatest contributors to making a lasting difference.

When we think of laughing and smiling, we equate feelings of happiness, gratitude, light-heartedness, contentment, purpose, freedom, peace and joy. And these emotions are also attributed to connections with people we love and who love us. These feelings are associated with provision and an overall satisfaction with life. So when life doesn't go our way, does that mean our happiness has to go with it?

The Financial Downer

When our finances were sparse and we had little

we could give or share, it affected my outlook on life, relationships and even took a toll on our marriage at times. When we are in lack, money can turn into the chain holding us back from our dreams. I remember a while back the lottery jackpot reached record-breaking numbers—a whopping 1.6 billion dollars for whoever held the winning ticket. People from every state were lined up at their local gas stations buying a chance at the jackpot. And for the few hours between their purchase and the drawing, people discussed wild ideas of what they would use the money for. People were going to start businesses, buy new houses, move to new cities, pay off debt, donate to charities or see the world. People who only days before couldn't dream past the end of their week, suddenly felt hope, vision and the freedom to get out of their small thinking. They could see a possibility for freedom, so they began to entertain the thought of a better tomorrow. You could ask them what they wanted to do, and for once, you wouldn't hear people talk about surviving at a nine-to-five job for the rest of their life. You would hear their dream. You would hear about their long-lost passion that they buried away because of the financial pressure. There's something much more sure and satisfying than the lottery to give your life real vision!

> "... When the LORD restored the fortunes of
> Zion, we were like those who dreamed."
> (Psalm 126:1)

God will restore our dreams if we will dream with Him and believe he is greater than any financial pressure. If we aren't careful, we can allow our finances to stop us from dreaming and enjoying life. We should dream like those people did waiting for the winning numbers to be announced because we already have the best jackpot there is—we have the Promises of God. That means we have every need supplied, to the point where we can be generous on every occasion (2 Corinthians 9:11). We have to dream of the endless possibilities we have with God.

There is certainly a correlation between being abundantly supplied and enjoying life with others. Money doesn't make for happiness, but having the ability to give to the ones you love and share happy times together do! When there is stress over finances or strain in relationships, we all feel less happy and become more negative in our outlook on life. But since everyone has to face pressures and relationship stressors in life, what is the one common, unchanging source of joy and happiness in life? What can keep our outlook positive when there are plenty of reasons to feel sad or discouraged? God's love and God's Word (or His will) for us become our joy because the joy of the Lord is our strength (Nehemiah 8:10).

Where Does Happiness Come From?

Having an attitude of gratitude toward God and others fosters positive feelings and keeps our focus on the good things in our life. Self-pity, disappointments and bitter attitudes have the opposite effect. According to a study from the John Templeton Foundation, the top five sources of gratitude in the U.S. are:

1. Our families

2. The freedoms of living in America

3. Good health

4. Close friends

5. Ability to practice religion

Notice that money was not in the list. Why? Because money is a tool that enhances these areas, but it doesn't create happiness.

Finding purpose, the comfort of prayer and building relationships in a community of church-based friends help bring positive feelings about life. It's crucial to our emotional well being to have friends and have positive exchanges with people around us.

"Study after study has found that religious people tend to be less depressed and less anxious than non-believers, better able to handle the vicissitudes of life than non-believers. A 2015 survey by researchers at the London School of Economics and Political Science and the Erasmus University Medical Center in the Netherlands found that participating in a religious organization was the only social activity associated with sustained happiness—even more than volunteering for a charity, taking educational courses or participating in a political or community organization." [2]

A lot of people are looking for something to satisfy them, going from one thing to the next—a hobby, a sport, a new boyfriend, girlfriend or relationship, a car or a

[2] TIME Magazine, The Science of Happiness: New Discoveries for a More Joyful Life

house. When you think about it, God has created so many wonderful opportunities for enjoyment. It's only when material things in life become misplaced in our hearts, our priorities get whacked out and instead of an added blessing, we make them the priority or focus to our own unhappiness.

Distraction #1: Putting Things First

Enjoying things is good and it is God's plan. He richly gives us all THINGS to enjoy! God's design and plan are to share an abundance of things with us as an overflow of His love just as we enjoy giving good gifts to our children. Why does He do this? Purely for our mutual enjoyment!

Interestingly enough, the world goes after money, success and things (lots of things!), but they will criticize believers and ministers who share the goodness of God in regards to things. They hypocritically call it a "prosperity gospel." Certainly the lust for things and the pride of life can choke love for God from the relationship, but if we seek Him first, His desire is to add the things of life to us. What happens in any relationship when things or self-ambition start to choke out sincere love and a mutual exchange? We lose our first love.

> *"As for the rich in this present age, charge them not to be haughty, nor to set their hopes on the uncertainty of riches, but on God, who richly provides us with everything to enjoy"*
> (I Timothy 6:17 ESV, author's emphasis).

> *"He satisfies your desires with good things so that your youth is renewed like the eagle's"*
> (Psalm 103:5, author's emphasis).

Things are <u>NOT</u> to be our source of joy. Hobbies are not what we give our life's purpose to. Go ahead and believe God for **things you need** and the **things you desire,** but seek Him first. The kingdom of God is not eating and drinking but righteousness and peace and joy in the Holy Spirit (Romans 14:17).

It is God's Spirit that brings us peace. That brings us joy. I like to think of the word "enjoy." I can't look to things to give me JOY. But if I am "in joy," in love with Jesus, THEN I am "in joy," and "In HIS JOY" I can enjoy things secondly.

We've all experienced misplaced priorities. When

Gary and I were living in Tulsa, Oklahoma, I was pregnant with our first child. I had gotten it into my head that having a baby meant owning our own home. We lived in a small apartment with furnishings that looked like they had barely survived the sixties. Avocado kitchen appliances and shag carpeting really "classed the place up!" And if that wasn't bad enough, our dining room table was a cardboard box I had flipped upside-down and covered with a tablecloth. If our living conditions were bad, they were only a reflection of our financial situation. I knew we didn't have the money to buy a house, but I thought if I had a house it would make me happier. I told Gary I didn't want to raise my baby on old shag carpets. I pushed the issue until we were in debt for a piece of property that was barely nicer than the apartment we came out of. And the funny part was, it had old shag carpet, too.

Shortly after I had the baby, Tulsa experienced a financial collapse. We were in debt and owed more on the house than it was worth. Now I was "in trouble" instead of "in joy," and I couldn't even "enjoy" the thing I thought would make me happy! In the meantime, God spoke to us both that we were to move to Columbus, Ohio, to do our end-time work. But how could we with an upside-down mortgage?

Thank God that when we get ourselves into trouble, He's there. We prayed and sought God FIRST, believing that He could move in the situation. I felt led to go meet with the banker and explained that our house wasn't worth what we owed on it. Looking at a stack of foreclosures 10 inches tall on her desk, she said, "We will appraise it and you can sell it for what it's worth. We'll write off the rest on insurance."

That was great news! There was only one problem: Nobody wanted to buy a house in Tulsa. More people were trying to get out of Tulsa than there were people sticking around! Factories were shutting down and jobs were becoming more and more scarce. In fact, moving companies had to *pay* people to drive all of the moving trucks back to the city. So where was I supposed to find a buyer? As an act of faith in God and seeking Him first, Gary and I gave a financial seed and committed to God that we would do whatever He was leading us to do for Him.

While watching Christian TV, I ran across Matthew 19:29: "And everyone who has left houses or brothers or sisters or father or mother or wife or children or fields for my sake will receive a hundred times as much with persecution and will inherit eternal life to come." I prayed and gave my house to God that morning. I let go! I recommitted the entire situation to Him and asked Him to sell it.

I had a peace and a joy in my heart that it was taken care of because I was no longer seeking things first. I had given this to God and He was back in the place of being my first love. I carefully wrote one ad and placed it in the newspaper, hosting an open house the following weekend. Many people came through our home but it only took the right one. On Monday I received a call from a woman who happened to be a believer and had a list of everything she wanted in a home. At the time she made the list, it looked impossible but she too had trusted God when a deal fell through the week before. Our house was everything she wanted, and she was in a position to pay cash!

When I told my banker the buyer didn't need to qualify because she had cash, I still remember her mouth dropping open and her exclaiming, "Where did you find this buyer?"

I told her!

As we sought God's plan, He did bring the promise we stood on about houses and land and blessings increasing in our life. And just as that scripture promises as well, people who continued to pursue things instead of seeking God first get jealous when they see you blessed, and some will persecute you. But that's a great reason to rejoice too. The scripture says (paraphrased), "Leap for joy, when you are persecuted for righteousness' sake" (Matthew 5:12).

You might ask, *who will persecute me?* People who are not willing to give up their way and seek Him first won't like it when they see you blessed because you put HIM first and HE blessed you. They will get jealous, and jealousy leads to persecution—which leads us to the next distraction that can steal joy from your heart . . . people-pleasing!

Distraction #2: Putting People's Approval First

Now certainly we want to get along with everybody and there are social graces and manners with proper behavior, but that's different than seeking people's approval. Choosing their approval over God's approval is the certain formula for losing your joy. Seeking people's approval won't bring joy—it will entrap you. Anything you seek more than you seek Him and His kingdom first will eventually cause you to lose your joy. When you look to Him first and seek His plan, His way, it will bless your life with plenty. The test is that when there aren't things or people to approve you, do you still know he is enough.

So if you haven't figured it out by now, living to please people is a trap. People that truly love you won't demand you to perform for them. If they are demanding you to perform for them, they are in love with themselves not you. And people that demand you perform what they want, or they will reject you, are still caught in the trap of insecurity. They can't love you or anyone else because it will always come back to their insecurity, needing you to do more or prove more.

Let's look at Jesus. He had healed bodies, praying, ministering and feeding the people around him. He did some nice things! But as soon as he didn't say or do what they wanted, they left him. Not just a few but most of them. He turned and asked the disciples if they would do the same. But the disciples had seen the other side of what Jesus did—the hardships, the sacrifice and his desire to help people. This all spoke to them and created a deeper relationship and commitment to Jesus. Peter said (paraphrased), "Lord, where would we go? You are the only one who has the words of eternal life" (John 6:68). They had seen too much to simply look at Jesus purely for what He could do for them. They hungered and thirsted for righteousness. Jesus sought first the Kingdom of God, and His joy was not based on popularity with the people. It didn't matter what others thought or who left. He was committed to pleasing the One He knew had called Him and to finish His assignment.

Gary and I had friends in college who we enjoyed being with because we shared a common vision of preparing ourselves for ministry and seeking God's plan for our life. And even though all of us were just barely making it by, we had purpose and dreams that fueled our enthusiasm and fun. Something began to change over a period of time though. The wife and mom of two children started working for a wealthy family, taking care of their home. It wasn't long before she started to compare her life to her employer's and became disenchanted with her pursuit of God and ministry, and mostly with her husband.

She lost a tremendous amount of weight and reinvented a life she admired. As her friend, I noticed her obsession with her new body, her money and the fact that she could now sport a crocheted string bikini. In her pursuit, she became distracted from her original purpose. Within a year, she and her family broke apart, ending her marriage and pursuing another relationship that she felt would make her happy—someone with more success and money. Her young children were devastated as she went on a journey to "find herself" and left them behind all alone.

Self-ambition and the pride of life will rob you of the peace of the Kingdom, of knowing Him. When you seek Him first, all things will be added. You will get satisfied. He will give you His ambitions for your life, and they will satisfy you. He will give you His THINGS for your life and they will be much better than all the THINGS you could manipulate, force, cheat or steal to get or make happen. Blessed are those who hunger and thirst for righteousness, for they will be satisfied. Which leads us to not just *what's* your first, but rather WHO'S YOUR FIRST?

Maybe you've sought things and it landed you in a world of debt, and today you don't find yourself any happier but backed up against a wall. Or maybe you've tried to please people and it's left you feeling alone or betrayed? Or running on a treadmill to keep up with somebody's demands who is never satisfied with you...that you can never do enough to make happy?

There is a SAVIOR from all the insanity and pressure of this world. He's offering peace and joy that you can be truly satisfied with. If you choose Him today—to hunger for His Kingdom—you will be satisfied with a joy that the world doesn't give and cannot take away.

Emotion Kick-start Challenge:

___ **Explore a new place.**

Find a change of scenery—whether it's a
local adventure, or a trip abroad. Enjoy a
new perspective on life from a place you've
never been. (The coffee shop down the
street counts.)

___ **Grab a meal with a friend.**

Make time to cultivate the relationships in
your life. Spending time with friends and
family is one of the quickest ways to meet
your happiness quota.

___ **Reward yourself.**

Schedule in some personal time, because
we all need it. And your friends and family
will thank you for taking it when they
experience the difference it makes in your
mood.

GOD-CONSCIOUS VS. SELF-CONSCIOUS

Chapter 8

I knew a very gifted and talented singer who had one of the best voices, yet whenever he stood before a crowd to share his gift, he became so self-conscious that he immediately forgot the words to the songs. His heart to sing for God was there, and so was the talent, but he was too self-conscious when he stood in front of people. Feelings of inadequacy and fears of failure robbed him of utilizing his God-given talent to lead others to focus on God in a worship setting. He lost his focus on God and it rendered his gift ineffective. Eventually he overcame this area of emotional weakness, stepping up and winning awards.

All talent and ability originate with God, our designer and creator. Learning to keep our eyes on the One who gave us certain abilities helps us develop a confidence that is greater than our limitations, strengths or weaknesses. If my confidence is in me, I can be manipulated with unworthiness or even pride, but if I am confident in the Lord, I am able to be used at His disposal and bring glory to Him. Insecurity and inadequacy result when I try to find identity and worth in my performance apart from Him. That's self-consciousness!

Earlier in our ministry days, a radio station invited me to share at a women's conference in the rolling hills of Amish country. My first invite of this kind, it was an honor and I wanted to do a great job for the station. As the conference grew closer, I was confronted in the hallway on a Sunday after service by one of the female members of our church. She said, "I've heard everything you have to say so I wasn't planning on attending the conference, but I decided God may want to use *me* there, so I decided to go." I thanked her for her decision and walked away. What words do you think stood out to me?

Her words, "I've heard everything you have to say," started to burn in my ears. Feelings took over, and I started to believe that my understanding and skills were so limited that I shouldn't be in the position to speak. I let those words replay over and over as the conference approached. I became focused on her evaluation instead of on the opportunity God had given me.

I prepared and prayed and really felt I had been given a word to share with these women, yet I was greatly hindered and fought feelings of fear and inadequacy mixed with offense. There was a tug of war going on inside me.

I was torn—insecurity and anxiety were winning over my desire to obey God by helping people.

The conference began and I took the platform. Just as I started my message, I caught a glance of the woman who had grabbed me in the hall, seated now in the back. When I saw her, her words began to ring loudly in my head. "I've already heard everything you have to say."

When I would start to share a story or make a point, my thoughts echoed, "They've heard it before. They've heard it before."

Trying to gather composure, I stumbled over my words, becoming more and more self-conscious. It wasn't an audible voice I heard, but it may as well have been since it seemed to be so loud in my head, I couldn't think straight. I felt total defeat and humiliation glancing over the faces of the crowd. Her words would have had little power over me were I not already insecure and feeling inadequate to speak.

The enemy of my soul had tapped into a tactic that worked against me, and for a time it was quite successful. There was a moment where it was unclear to me whether I would make it through the session or not, but there was no escape. I had to face my fear and myself.

Verbally tripping on words, awkwardly, I shifted to ask the women to join me in prayer. Prayer is my strength! In that moment I turned my thoughts and feelings off, submitted myself to God, and the power of His Spirit filled the auditorium. A grace forcefully unleashed in such a way that I felt as if something apprehended me, and I spoke words that were not my own. Before I knew it I was finished and offering prayer for those who came forward. Women lined up for prayer, and it was evident that God took over where I could not.

The woman who had confronted me in the hall was one of the last of so many women who came forward. She was almost being dragged down by the two other women leading her, and I had the privilege of praying for her. The spirits of insecurity controlling her had attempted to overpower me too, but God prevailed when I became God-conscious instead of self-conscious.

The inadequacy and fear she felt had intimidated me because I possessed familiar feelings of insecurity that she tapped into. The tactic worked at least temporarily against me because I lacked the understanding that my real source of frustration and attack was spiritual and required spiritual weapons to combat it. It took me some time to discover I was not wrestling with flesh and blood, but rather with powers and principalities that wanted to stop me (and this woman) from obedience to God. Satan used this tactic until I was no longer ignorant of his scheme. If he could get me to become self-conscious, performance-driven based out of fear or a need to secure myself, I would consistently be defeated.

BECOME GOD-CONSCIOUS
(What He Says and Who He Is)

NOT

SELF-CONSCIOUS
(Your Past, Your Failures)

The Pride Problem

I have discovered apart from God I can do nothing, but with Him, I can do all things. Jesus said, "I am the true vine and you are the branches. Apart from me, you can do nothing" (John 15). If we try to put our confidence in our performance, then it is completely up to us to pull off what must be done. "God opposes the proud but gives grace to the humble"

(James 4:6). I want God's grace in life, for it is the power to do far more than I could ever accomplish in my own effort.

Most people are attempting to get their identity from their performance or paycheck to "become" somebody. In God's Kingdom, you and I *are* somebody! And when we discover who we are in Christ and what we have in Him, we can do great things. We don't attempt great things to become somebody; we attempt great things *because* we are somebody! When our identity becomes secure in Him, and His love and grace in our life, limitations are replaced with strength, boldness and power to do all things in Christ.

We can be born into God's Kingdom and still miss out on our freedom in Christ. Quite easily we go from performing works in the world for identity to performing in the church for the same. Self-ambition and the pride of life are hidden traps that will hinder our successful walk in Christ. They are a form of pride and self-protection because we lack trust and submission to God. "Do nothing out of self-ambition and vain conceit. Rather, in humility value others above yourselves" (Philippians 2:3). Humbling myself to receive His grace (His ability) causes me to power up to the potential He placed in me, and it works the same for you too. It's "'not by might nor by power, but by My Spirit,' says the Lord" (Zechariah 4:6). Recognizing our need for God instead of relying on self-sufficiency or independence—gives you and me great grace. The more we trust Him, the greater His grace. "My grace is sufficient for you, for my power is made perfect in weakness" (2 Corinthians 12:9). What a wonderful discovery—when we are weak, He is strong. We get out of the way and let Him take control.

I've since encountered these same spirits of jealousy and insecurity on many occasions working with people. By the way, insecurity and jealousy operate together because if we don't know who we are, we tend to get envious of who someone else is!

The Voice of Insecurity

I don't always get it right, but the enemy's tactics move me far less now. Once I quit giving voice to insecurity in my emotional realm, it stopped being effective against me; the enemy withdrew ceasing to control me through people's evaluations and attitudes. Maturity starts when we entrust ourselves into God's hands even when people mistreat or misunderstand us or become a weapon against our destiny.

This played out in business on several occasions as well. My husband is a hard worker, but through the years we hired a few people in our sales company that weren't! Inevitably the more someone talked about how great they were or how big they were going to build the business, the less they performed and the more they complained and blamed us. Big talkers became suspect! They often lacked the emotional stability or security in Christ to actually do what they said, and when their success was minimal, they blamed Gary. On one such occasion, I remember we had a self-evaluation time. Struggling with feelings of defeat and inadequacy, it suddenly dawned on us, *why are we lamenting over this*? We have a proven track record that the business works quite well! Why should we allow someone not producing to stop us or take the joy of hard-earned success from us? We could have helped them if they would have been humble and teachable; with Gary's successful track record he could have mentored them. Unfortunately, pride and teachable attitudes don't usually coexist. How much time have you wasted worrying over the evaluations of critical people? Are you allowing their choices to keep you from your destiny?

When we are self-conscious, our mind plays tricks on us, and combined together with feelings of insecurity, this is a combination for discouragement and defeat. Turn the table on the enemy by acknowledging, "apart from Him (God), you can do nothing." And at the same breath, recognize and declare boldly, "I can do all things THROUGH Christ because He gives me the strength." (See Philippians 4:13.) In the face of criticism, humbly accept that you are not able to do it, but God in you can!

It has been said that the mind is the battlefield. If the mind is where the battle occurs, emotions are the gatekeepers guarding the mind and providing the necessary ammunition to keep the war of conflicting beliefs going. When the belief system is challenged with God's Word, not only must we choose God's Word as the truth, we will need to deal with emotional triggers and responses to break free.

For instance, emotional wounds often precede chronic sickness. In thirty-plus years of ministry involvement, I have observed a pattern in chronically sick people of strongholds especially in the areas of unforgiveness, unworthiness, self-pity or a craving for attention that sickness may afford its victims. Sickness can become an escape and an insulating force—a desperate cry for attention they feel would not be garnered without the illness. Certainly this is not always the case, but it is a familiar pattern. Emotionally wounded or neglected people may subconsciously use sickness as a way to get time and attention when all else fails.

Feelings and emotional scars guard the gates to the heart, keeping the person from the truth that would set them free. Perhaps this is why Jesus said, "Would you be made whole?" or "What can I do for you?" Even though their sickness was evident, as He confronted their physical pain or disease, He had to get past their emotions and belief system to locate whether they "would (allow themselves to) be made whole." Rehearsing hurts will keep the body in a state of sickness. If healing and forgiveness are not applied like a balm to the soul, then broken hearts will accompany broken bodies. Jesus came to heal the brokenhearted and with it, damaged emotions. In the area of sickness, we can choose to be God-conscious or self-conscious as well.

The Word of God is medicine to the flesh, but bitterness is rottenness to the bones (Proverbs 14:30). When we are no longer emotionally led but rather spirit-led, our level of victorious living propels us to a new place! "No longer are we children tossed to and fro by every wind..." (See Ephesians 4:14).

Surrender is a beautiful word. If we choose to surrender our will, emotional pain and confusion to His Word, we become more conscious of His Word than life's wounds, and we can be made whole. Whether it's confidence, physical healing or provision of any kind, He sent His Word and delivered us from all our pain (Isaiah 53). When we believe this and allow our emotions to be delivered from all oppression, the emotional guards leave and we can receive bodily healing too. Renewing the mind to God's picture creates faith and faith brings results! Letting God's Word not only renew your mind but also possess your soul will bring the will to fight sickness and the emotional strength to be free.

Let's become GOD-CONSCIOUS (what He says, who He is, and who He says we are) INSTEAD of being SELF-CONSCIOUS (focused on our past, our failures or sickness). God's Word must become the authority in your life. Whether you realize it or not, every time you hear God's Word, you make a conscious decision whether to believe and accept it as your truth or not. If you are self-focused, you will reject what God says and let your memories tell you your future. If you choose to make what God says your focus, then you can change your belief system! Changing your belief system will change your life! Guaranteed!

Emotion Kick-start Challenge:

Fill out this self-evaluation:

___ Do I tend to be more self-conscious or God-conscious? Why?

___ What emotional hot buttons do I allow Satan to use to defeat me? (e.g., anger, offenses, insecurity, unworthiness, self-pity, rashness, pride)

___ What unhealthy relationships are controlling me rather than God?

___ How will I change my response to these people?

___ Have I surrendered to God and allowed myself to be teachable instead of prideful?

MISERY LOVES COMPANY

Chapter 9

To renew our mind and stay anchored to God's Spirit gives our lives a firm foundation. Emotions are defined as a state of mind derived from one's *circumstances, mood* or *relationships* with others. Clearly our state of mind can be altered by situations, and our mood can be erratic depending on how much sleep we've had, how much money is in our checking account or how nice someone was or wasn't to us. Because our emotional state can be easily altered by circumstances, it can play tricks and deceive us into hardening ourselves against the very answers we need.

Sadly, marketers and politicians have learned to manipulate emotions to move people to make decisions that are not always in their best interests. I consistently watch politicians divide voters using discrimination and political correctness as a carrot. Meanwhile the people holding the carrot often have the worst track records for bringing real change or answers to our communities. Their livelihood is built around creating division, not solving the problems. They have learned the art of emotionally angering people to get their focus off what is really happening. The resulting emotion becomes a diversion to detract from the facts.

Marketers can use division to move us as well. When you see an ad for a vacation that you can charge on a credit card, it's easy to become divided between your commitment to get out of debt and the desire for what you see in the ad! This division becomes double-mindedness and causes you to lose the will to stick with your original goal.

Satan also knows how to play on our emotions, setting us up for conflicts in our soul and offenses with others that can end in separation and division. He baits us with offenses to divide and conquer. It is not flesh and blood that you wrestle with, but powers, principalities, might and dominion and everything that sets itself up against the knowledge of God's Word (Ephesians 6:12). We must wake up to his tactics and stop being tossed around like children who are naïve and easily tricked by bad guys. This requires emotional maturity developed by training in God's Word, and it requires humility and our choice to be teachable.

Too many times people blame God for hardships in their lives when oftentimes it is the work of our own hearts that create our problems. Offenses or holding grudges, which is a form of unforgiveness, account for calloused hearts and lead us to betray. We have all been betrayed, and we have all betrayed someone.

I know a pastor who shared with me how he almost left the ministry over a wounded heart in his early days. He had a tender heart toward people and especially toward a couple who helped him in the beginning days of his church as a friend and leader. Over a period of time this couple went through some hardships and made decisions that opened the door to a calloused heart toward the minister. They became offended and after a series of issues, they left the church and the pastor who cared greatly for them. The pastor was so deeply hurt in his inexperience he wanted to quit, blaming himself for the failure. God spoke to him and said that they had betrayed Him and the church, and to let them go. The pastor managed to continue on in ministry after recognizing that his own heart must be single-purposed to follow God. He said it was the hardest thing he had ever been through, but many years later, this couple returned. This time they returned with a different heart—a heart that was humble and willing to admit their wrong. They shared how many years of turmoil had cost them family relations, finances and other church problems. They had come with a repentant heart and ready to make things right. The relationship was restored, and the couple became active again in the church. This pastor was so grateful to see everything come full circle. Unfortunately this is not always how the story ends.

We all have tendencies to find fault in others and use those faults to justify our own wrongdoing, but this doesn't fly with God. Just like the Israelites circled through the wilderness for years when God had promised them a land of abundance, many believers are wandering around disconnected from God's leadership, blessings and provision because of offenses and wounds. Ministers have left their posts, and disciples have stopped their support of leadership. This tactic of Satan to divide and conquer has greatly damaged hearts and ministries. It's time to reconcile differences and see the big picture, which is more important than foolish arguments that create strife. It's time to come into a place of maturity in Christ and the abundance that comes with obedience.

Pride: The Ultimate Blinder

Pride is the protector of all evils in our hearts and lives. When we can humbly admit we were wrong, we can change and bring change. "If my people who are called by name will humble themselves and pray...I will heal their land" (2 Chronicles 7:14). Why are we afraid to admit we are wrong and afraid to receive healing? Wounded emotions. When we are mistreated or experience injustice, we have two choices: to forgive and let God take our case or to retain the offense and take up our own case with a personal vengeance to get even. One requires humility, and the other is based in stubborn pride. Pride causes us to fall over ourselves literally. It's like stumbling over your own foot. Pride becomes the guard at the gate of our heart, and wounded emotions are on the inside. Those wounds need healed so we can receive all that God has, but if we keep pride guarding the door to our heart, how can God's healing get in?

> John 9:41 says, *"If you were blind, you wouldn't be guilty,' Jesus replied. 'But you remain guilty because you claim you can see.'"* (NLT)

Throughout years of counsel and pastoral leadership, I've witnessed people harm themselves and their family to protect their pride. God can give grace to humble people, but a proud person He casts out. Why? You can't teach a proud person anything. They think they are right and will fight to prove it and to prove you wrong. They may think they've won the battle, but in the long run they lose the war. They're the only ones who can't see it even though it becomes evident to those around them impacting business negotiations, finances, spiritual growth and relationships.

When Dealing with Offenses:

1. Talk to the person you have an issue with and not with others about the person or situation. If you have an issue or fault with your brother, GO TO HIM, not around him.

2. Don't take up others' offenses and become a third party in the middle of a concern or conflict. Third parties lose. Rightfully, the scripture says to mind your own business and lead a peaceable life. (See 1 Thessalonians 4:11.) There is no peace when you try to take false responsibility for situations that don't involve you.

3. Don't stuff feelings down inside unless you want them to explode when you least expect it.

Maturity in our emotions and fruitfulness happens when we can admit our failings, receive counsel, and hold our actions to the standard of God's Word rather than justifying ourselves and blaming others.

That leads me to a discussion about blame. If you have lived in an atmosphere where you were shamed or ridiculed for making mistakes, especially if you were belittled, then you likely have developed a performance, law-based belief system. You could be very critical and have difficulty accepting responsibility when you make a mistake. Your wounds have taught you that to be wrong or to make a mistake is unacceptable and grounds for utter rejection and separation from love. None of us can live without love, so if admitting we are wrong means we are unworthy of love, then we can't admit wrong. Do you see what a circular trap this is? If I can't admit I'm wrong, I can't get help; but I fear admitting I'm wrong if it means I'm not worthy to be loved. This is Satan's lie. It's a counterfeit belief system from what God says about love and humility.

The act of humbling ourselves to admit we have made mistakes opens the door to forgiveness, restoration and healing! We have all been wrong. We have all fallen short of God's standard. Who can say they are perfect? Self-righteousness or performance-based righteousness will always leave us spiritually bankrupt with either pride over our good performance or shame over our poor performance, and either one is a miserable measure of our identity.

When people come to Gary or me offended with something they heard in a message we shared, we try to hear what they say but also let the Holy Spirit unveil what is behind what they say. Typically, one of three scenarios happens. The first: I admit I may have said something wrong, which requires me to ask for their forgiveness. The second: Sometimes they misunderstood what was intended, which further communication can clarify. The third: Sometimes they have a wound that keeps them from hearing without offense what was said. It's exactly the medicine for the wound they have nursed, sometimes for many years. Because pride is guarding the door to their heart, it's hard to hear that truth. It's like there's a prison around their heart and pride is guarding the door. Proverbs 18:19 says, "An offended friend is harder to win back than a fortified city. Arguments separate friends like a gate locked with bars." (NLT) Truth is trying to break down the pride and get inside and set them free from their prison. Pride guards the door fervently shutting out the answer. Sometimes they break through the wall and humbly receive the truth that is able to save them. Other times, they resist the medicine the Holy Spirit is trying to get to them to heal their wounds so they can receive the answers they have cried out to Him for.

It's a delicate situation and if you've been in it, you understand why Paul said in 2 Timothy 2:25, "Gently instruct those who oppose the truth. Perhaps God will change those people's hearts, and they will learn the truth themselves that by chance they may be won over." (NLT) I'm sorrowful if they go away hardening themselves even more. I know that I am accountable for my words and heart and I ask God to teach me; they are accountable if they heard truth and rejected it. We must all remain teachable. All I can offer someone is God's answers from His Word, to be the best example I can be, and when I fall short, to humbly seek God's help. It's all easier said than done, but we can't learn anything if we think we know all the answers. I don't know it all. You don't, but He does.

Malachy McCourt said, "Resentment is like taking poison and waiting for the other person to die."

Another minister shared a story with us while we were in an airport on the way to teach at a church. He spoke with a lady who said she had previously attended the church that he was scheduled to speak at. She went on to share how God had healed her of a life-threatening disease while she attended there. When he asked her why she no longer attended, she said she disagreed with the leaders and left. How many offenses are working against lives of believers? We are instructed to stay out of strife 'for where envying and strife is, there is confusion and every evil work. (James 3:16 KJV) We must guard our heart from offense and not blame God when there's a problem. Instead, let's examine our own hearts, submit ourselves to correction from the Holy Spirit and then stop the enemy's attack. "Submit ... to God. Resist the devil and he will flee from you." (James 4:7)

A Defense Against Offense

Ultimately we must trust God and open our hearts to the Holy Spirit, clinging to God's Word and love over all other voices or responses. Offenses are the tactics Satan uses to get us to close down, oftentimes to our own answer. We see this in operation in Jesus' hometown where people exclaimed, "All his sisters live right here among us. Where did he learn all these things? And they were deeply offended and refused to believe in him..." (Matthew 13:56-57 NLT). **They were too familiar with Jesus—the man—to accept Him as their God-sent answer.** It is truth from God that will set us free, but if we have invested in a lie or clung to a falsehood, pride can make us offended at the very truth we need to hear, and also at the messenger God chooses to use.

If something angers me I have to rewind and ask myself, *what is the root of my response?* Is it grounded in facts, feelings or false beliefs? Is it something I need to hear to help me see a better way? We all think we are right until we are convicted that perhaps we have believed something wrong. That's why God's Word can be the only standard or we are mistakenly led into deception. It is obvious that as America has departed more and more from God's Word, error and division have set up strongholds in our nation and robbed all Americans of His best for our country.

Satan is the father of lies and division in the Body of Christ. He managed to split heaven and get a third of the angels to rebel against God. His divisive tactics can be witnessed from the courthouse to the home. The soul realm and primarily emotions are the place of attack because when a person's emotions take the driver's seat, all rational thinking or biblical definition of right or wrong are often thrown out the window! Emotions are erratic drivers that swerve all over the road and easily lose focus on facts or truth.

If we want to walk as Jesus did in the Spirit of truth and not error, we must let God's Word drive the car of our life and let our emotions take the back seat. When our spirit man, submitted to God, drives the car, emotions can add fuel, fun and energy to the drive, but we should never put emotions in the driver's seat. Ask yourself when tempted to lose self-control, who is in the driver's seat? Stop and switch drivers if you have let emotions jump in there and push out the Spirit from controlling the car of your life!

Step 6: *Examine your heart and ask, "Am I a teachable person? Do I need to be right all of the time?"*

Emotion Kick-start Challenge:

Fill out this self-evaluation form:

___ **What offense with a person may be hindering my ability to hear an answer I need?**

___ **What area do I need help but may be closed like a gate to instruction? (e.g., finances, marriage, parenting, spiritual guidance)**

___ **How do I handle correction from my boss or a church leader?**

OVERCOMING
DISCOURAGEMENT

Chapter 10

When we are weighted down with cares, worries or fears, a spirit of heaviness can bind up the mind and emotions, making it hard to see past discouraging feelings and depressing thoughts. Loneliness, the loss of a loved one or trauma from a major setback can bring so many overwhelming feelings of pain, guilt, regret and remorse that it may seem impossible to rise above them. The very foundation of a person's belief system is shaken to the core and hopelessness is their companion instead of faith. This is how heaviness weighs on the heart and mind with grief and deep sorrow until it becomes a stronghold choking out life and all joy. But there is great hope regardless of how people may feel in the darkest times; we are not alone.

Our spirit was designed by God to rule our life. Just as our natural body needs nourishment to grow, our spirit needs to be fed the Word of God to maintain faith and lead our lives. What we feed grows, and what we neglect withers. The parable of the sower says that the Word is sown into our hearts but immediately the enemy comes to steal the Word—to choke it out with persecution, troubles, cares, lust for things and the deceitfulness of riches. When the planting of God's Word is choked out, other weeds grow and begin to oppress our soul. Our mind becomes burdened with care and negative news, and our emotions get so down we lose hope. Add to this feeling a focus on personal shortcomings with guilt, and you have the recipe for depression. This is the picture of heaviness that gets a stronghold on the mind and emotions, leading to a depressed state.

What is the answer to breaking free from the spirit of heaviness? Since we know it is a spirit according to scripture, we must address it as such. There is practical help and professional counsel, but also dealing with the spiritual realm is the answer to long-term freedom. The Holy Spirit is our comforter and companion. God has sent him to come beside us and help us, and especially in times of great need. He will never leave us or forsake us so we are never truly alone! Recognize that God is not only with you, He is for you! It's important to recognize that grief and feelings of loneliness will not last forever. When heaviness is present it seems like there's no future and maybe no reason to continue but when all hope is gone and feelings have displaced faith by painting a bleak picture, God is still with you. He will never leave you or forsake you regardless of how you may feel.

It's important to separate feelings from facts using scripture as your absolute truth and rebuild your spiritual foundation that has been shaken by circumstances. Because emotions are so strong, our losses can seem permanent, but it's just not true. Earth has no sorrow that heaven cannot heal. We must make a solid choice using our will that we believe God is our refuge and strength and He is a very present help in times of trouble. In trouble, we must choose to stop trying to make sense of things mentally, stop replaying what happened, release the pain and give it all to God. Persons in deep grief and sorrow will often say, "I just can't." I understand that feeling, and it's true you can't, but the Holy Spirit given to every believer on the inside of you can!

Step 7: *Let go and let God take control of your life. That's freedom!*

We are instructed to put on the garment of praise for the spirit of heaviness. (See Isaiah 61:3.) Praise declares the goodness of God and lifts us from despair into a place of hope. We can't stay in a place of defeat if we are focused on God's victory. Just as Paul and Silas faced a seemingly hopeless situation after being flogged and thrown into prison (Acts 16), it was their choice to praise God in the midst of oppressing trouble that changed them, their countenance and their circumstances. They were delivered from within and then change came outwardly too. The earth quaked; the chains were broken off of them and their cell door opened, freeing them to get back on assignment. Not only were they delivered, but they were able to lead the jailer and his family into the same freedom. (See Acts 16:25-34.)

We have been given authority over all the power of the enemy and nothing can remain the same when we praise God. Our praise is a weapon to stop the enemy and end his escapade. Praising God while in trouble is an action that releases faith. It takes faith to stand up and declare God's faithfulness and goodness when the situation doesn't seem to warrant it and you don't have all the answers.

In Judges 6, Joshua and the people of God began to praise God marching around the city, and the walls of their adversary came down just like Paul and Silas experienced. We know that God inhabits the praises of His people.

Conversely, satanic activity has access when we declare the problem instead of praising the One with the answer, our Creator, the maker of heaven and earth. Heaviness is not God's plan for our lives. His yoke is easy and His burden is light. (See Matthew 11:30.) Refuse to let care and worry be your companions and weigh down your life. "Rejoice in the Lord always; again I say rejoice!" (Philippians 4:4 NASB). In this world there is trouble, but be of good cheer, Jesus has overcome it. Since He overcame, you overcome too.

Pray this:

Father, I take authority over all oppression and break the spirit of heaviness off of my life. Grief and sorrow, leave me! I will not be discouraged, depressed or weighed down with cares. I cast all my care on You God because You care for me. I choose to think on things that are lovely, of a good report and I rejoice in the Lord! Holy Spirit, I receive your comfort and your help in time of trouble. Fill me with your power and great grace to rise above these situations in my life I learn to walk with Jesus in victory and joy for I am yoked with Him and He carries me in this time. My burden is light. I refuse to carry what Jesus already carried. I refuse to grieve any longer. Sorrow and mourning go from me. I am free! I am free from weights and my heart is light. Walls come down and joy burst forth in the Name of Jesus!

Put on a praise album! It's time to do a happy dance! Praise God and celebrate your victory over guilt, sin, shame and all of Satan's tactics. You are free!

Emotion Kick-start Challenge:

___ **Do something that makes you laugh.**

> Watch a funny movie, see a comedian or invest time into doing something that makes you giggle. Put laughter on your daily to-do list.

___ **Volunteer time doing for others.**

> Serve your community locally or help out a friend. Whether it's a big or small task, we feel happier when we are spreading happiness!

___ **Smile.**

> Wear a smile as if it was clothing and you'd be naked without it. Observe how it affects your emotions and the way people treat you.

A GUILTY PLEASURE

Chapter 11

Guilt is intended to bring remorse or conviction so that true change can occur, but if harbored, it becomes destructive and results in shame.

Step 8: *Refuse to rehearse the past and let go of regret.*

Fear, insecurity and guilt entered mankind the day that Adam and Eve chose to rebel against God's Word and counsel from a loving Father. Guilt is defined as the fact of having committed a specified or implied offense or crime. The response to wrongful action is feelings of guilt, or you could say a conscience that convicts us of our behavior. It was more than just a decision to eat from the tree in disobedience; it was a choice to kick God out of the driver seat of their life—to take control and do as they pleased. All wrongdoing is rooted in the same self-centered lust for something unlawful. God has supplied a right way, or righteous way, to live life; and when we choose to violate his plan, it is sin. Anything that is not of faith is sin. Sin brings guilt.

A culture's conscience becomes seared when it can no longer feel or admit wrong and instead justifies evil in the guise of something good. That's exactly the argument that Satan used in the Garden. He enticed Eve with promises of a better life if she chose a different way than what God instructed her. It sounded good to have the power and knowledge of God that he promised her. After all, if she could be like God, she could be powerful. Interestingly, Satan tempted her with something she already had! She and Adam were made in God's image and likeness and had been given dominion and rule over the earth. God had already endowed them with all He had, so it was really a power struggle no different than when Satan rebelled against God in heaven. "I will exalt myself above the throne of God," Lucifer (Satan) stated (Isaiah 14:14). Eve was promised the same. She convinced her husband and they both fell into the guilt and shame of sin.

Feelings of guilt are to help us recognize that what we have done is wrong and to seek reconciliation with those we have harmed—to make things right. The human response to guilt is to hide, and that's exactly what Adam and Eve did when they listened to the deception of Satan and exchanged their freedom for the torment of guilt.

A Dead-end Street

The process of sin looks something like this:

SIN

GUILT

HIDING

BLAMING

SHAMING

HARDNESS

<u>BONDAGE</u>

When God confronted their rebellion, Eve said, "The serpent tricked me...," and Adam said, "[The] woman you gave me..." (Genesis 3:12-13 NET). They both blamed someone else for their decision to rebel. This isn't something we have to be taught to do! Have you seen those YouTube videos of small children making excuses, even blaming dolls or toys for the crime? We were born with this very same nature to blame someone or justify ourselves; when we do wrongly but excuse ourselves or blame others, our judgments place us in a cycle of defeat. Shame is the outcome.

Eventually if we stay in this cycle of sin, the heart becomes calloused and hard. The Bible records that Judas could not find a place of repentance after he betrayed Jesus. He hardened his heart with every plot and action to harm Jesus. He justified his behavior indignantly, accusing Jesus of mishandling money when the woman poured out her fragrant perfume on His feet. He kept finding fault with Jesus to justify Himself. People will often judge others by the hidden sin in their own hearts. Judas eventually plotted to hand Him over, but really he handed himself over to Satan in the process. His life ended by suicide, as he no longer could find a place of repentance or the way to turn from his calloused heart.

Whenever we sin or break the law, we feel guilt. God gave laws to his people to bring them to a place of repentance or turning from evil and to prevent their hearts from becoming calloused past hearing His call. We can justify our good behavior and try to put it on a scale to weigh it against our bad behavior, or perhaps we could try putting our sins on a scale and weighing them against someone else's sin to attempt to justify ourselves, but at the end of the day we are all guilty. James 2:10 states, "For the person who keeps all of the laws except one is as **guilty** as a person who has broken all of God's laws" (NLT).

Remaining in a state of guilt would be a terrible place to end, but it's not the end! Father God was not interested in condemning us but instead wanted to lead us to a guilt-less life of freedom in Christ.

Choosing a Different Path

Step 9: *Allow conviction to bring repentance so repentance can bring change.*

Romans 5:16 encourages us, "And the result of God's gracious gift is very different from the result of that one man's sin. For Adam's sin led to condemnation, but God's free gift leads to our being made right with God, even though we are **guilty** of many sins" (NLT).

Not only did God make things right as a free gift, but He also encourages us to trust Him enough to boldly run to Him, not away from Him so HE can wash our hearts and consciences clean. "Let us go right into the presence of

God with sincere hearts fully trusting him. For our **guilty** consciences have been sprinkled with Christ's blood to make us clean, and our bodies have been washed with pure water" (Hebrews 10:22 NLT).

God is inviting us to fully trust Him with the guilt we feel and let Christ's blood eradicate it. Trust means I put my confidence in His ability, His love and the sacrifice of Jesus instead of trusting in my performance. Regardless of our mistakes, whether intentional, premeditated or accidental, He has a plan of restoration because of His great love for us—and we can trust that!

SIN

GUILT

CONVICTION

CONFESSION

REPENTANCE

FORGIVENESS

RESTORATION

<u>FREEDOM</u>

God's Spirit will convict us of all wrongdoing, and then we confess it and much like an eraser, it removes it from our retention to His justification and removal of sin. If we confess our sins, He is faithful and just to cleanse us from all unrighteousness. (See 1 John 1:9.) Repentance is to turn from sin and walk a different path instead of the one that brought you to a dead end street.

Condemnation is based in unforgiveness and characterized by feelings of hopelessness and regret. In order to move forward, stop rehearsing the guilt of past mistakes.

God never intended for you to carry guilt. You can't carry sin without eternal consequences; that's why Jesus had to carry it to the cross. Guilt will destroy your relationship with God and others, your confidence and your physical well-being! But how many believers are still rehearsing their failures, living in a world of regret?

Forward Thinking

Where you are going is much more important than where you've been, but if you determine to look and focus backwards, you will keep yourself in a state of regret and pain.

I like to break down REGRET into this acronym:

R – REHEARSING
E – EVERY
G – GRIEVANCE
R – RUINS
E – EVERY
T – TODAY (AND TOMORROW!)

The enemy would love to keep you and me on a pathway of regret. It is a hopeless, condemned place of recounting and renaming all our wrongs and living in a place of utter defeat. You may have to pay restitution for your wrongdoing to others, but as far as God is concerned, you have been fully restored to a place of relationship and rights in His Kingdom. Don't let guilt rob you of your citizenship and inheritance in Christ. Your future is calling you. Will you let go of yesterday's pain and answer today's call?

Step 10: *Learn from mistakes but refuse feelings of condemnation.*

I love what 1 John 3:20 says,
"Even if we feel guilty, God is greater than our feelings, and he knows everything" (NLT, author's emphasis).

Isn't that wonderful! Let that sink in. God knows everything about us, and He wants to encourage us that He is greater than our feelings. You can feel guilty, but God is greater! Let go of the feelings and trust God has greater than what you may feel.

G – GIVING
U – UNWORTHINESS AND
I – INSECURITY
L – LICENSE TO
T – TORMENT

Guilt is perhaps one of the greatest areas we must not succumb to feelings in. Your enemy would love nothing more than to keep you from coming to Christ but once you have, his second line of defense is to rob you of all faith or confidence in God's Word and His ability in you, and ultimately the authority you possess in Christ over Satan. How can you free others and be a light in the world if you are under condemnation and regret by carrying the guilt of past mistakes? Unresolved guilt will try to bind you to unworthiness and feelings of insecurity. Unworthiness reminds us we fall short and tries to convince us we are not worthy of love. Insecurity drives us to a performance mindset that convinces us we are inadequate because of our sin. But that's not what God says about us once we have received the sacrifice of Jesus as a guilt offering!

The Word of God says you have been seated with Christ in heavenly places. (Ephesians 2:6.) You are not under Satan's dominion. Jesus has seated you next to Him, and Satan is under His feet. Each morning, get in your seat right next to Jesus! It's a place of righteousness in Christ and authority over the enemy. See yourself seated above sin, guilt, principalities, power, might and dominion. See yourself washed from a guilty conscience, free from accusation. You may have fallen for a lie or trick of the enemy, but don't make the second mistake of falling for condemnation. We must run quickly to the throne where we will find ourselves wrapped in Daddy's arms of love and covering of grace.

> *There is NO condemnation to those who are in Christ Jesus.* (Romans 8:1)

Avoiding the Trap

Satan is the accuser of the brethren and he is out to

point the finger of accusation. Pain seeks to find pleasure to cover or escape. If we don't let Christ cleanse us from guilt, then guilt will drive us like a slave to sin again and again, producing greater guilt and pain and eventually hardness. But when we recognize how loved, accepted and cared for we are, we can let Father God's forgiveness free us from chronic sin. Renew your thoughts to what God says about you and who you are in Him.

Righteousness, or being made right, is a gift from God and once you receive it, there is no benefit in rehearsing your sin and being sin-conscious. Instead, start declaring who you are in Christ and identify with His righteousness. Religion encourages people to wallow in sin-consciousness, but that actually holds people captive to sin when we are no longer held guilty by sin. We've been set free from a prison sentence, yet instead of declaring our freedom, too often we stay in captivity by carrying the emotional baggage of guilt.

So what do we do if we sin as a believer? I John 1:9 says that if we confess our sin, He is faithful and just to forgive us and to cleanse us from all unrighteousness. He already chose to forgive us on the cross when He said,

"Father forgive them." But when we confess, it's for our benefit to clear ourselves from guilt and clean our heart and conscience so we can stay free.

Recognize the difference between conviction, which leads us to repentance for our benefit, and condemnation that leads to feelings of hopelessness, shame, regret and defeat. God's Spirit will encourage you toward a pathway of recovery and restoration. Condemnation for the believer is a lying, deceptive spirit and comes from the evil one. Only the devil and his angels, together with those who have rejected the sacrifice of Jesus for their freedom, are condemned. "Then will He say to those at His left, "'Be gone from me, with the curse resting upon you, into the Fire of the Ages, which has been prepared for the Devil and his angels...'" (Matthew 25:41 Weymouth)

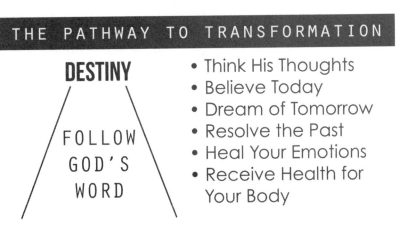

THE PATHWAY TO TRANSFORMATION

DESTINY

FOLLOW
GOD'S
WORD

- Think His Thoughts
- Believe Today
- Dream of Tomorrow
- Resolve the Past
- Heal Your Emotions
- Receive Health for Your Body

If you will let go of yesterday and answer today's call, your life will undergo a transformation! Your **destiny** can begin today with the simple decision to think His thoughts, to believe what He says today and to let yourself dream His big dreams for your tomorrow. Resolve the past and let God bring healing to your emotions and throw off the weights and emotional baggage. Hebrews 12:1 says, "Therefore, since we are surrounded by such a great cloud of witnesses, let us throw off everything that hinders and the sin that so easily entangles. And let us run with perseverance the race marked out for us." The side effect to your emotional health is it will bring healing to your body as well!

CHOOSE YOUR PATH

Choose today what to focus on!
Direct your life!
Choose YOUR desitiny!

YESTERDAY'S PAIN   TOMORROW'S DREAM

So how do we resolve yesterday's pain and move away from regrets? It comes back to our thoughts and emotions! Every day of your life, you must CHOOSE whether you think on yesterday or dream about tomorrow. Choose today what to FOCUS ON. Decide to not let feelings rule your life. Choose your destiny by making a choice TODAY. I used to have a sign on our bathroom wall that said, "Make the choice to rejoice." Whenever I was upset I would lock myself in the bathroom to cry, but that sign helped me CHOOSE how I was going to manage my life, AND more importantly, HOW I was going to MANAGE my emotions and the circumstances that brought tears. I moved on from that environment, and our life was transformed by what we chose in the difficult times. CHOOSE YOUR DESTINY! CHOOSE your thinking! The past can look ugly, so how can I think right about it? I can't deny it happened and I can't deny the mistakes, but I can proclaim that I am free, and who the Son sets free is free indeed! I can choose to resolve that I do not have to live in regret, but I can live free because of what God in His Love has done for me. And you can too! One of the best ways to do this is to make declarations over yourself of who you are in Christ Jesus. Identify the lies and find scripture to refute them. Replace condemnation with victorious words.

Emotion Kick-start Challenge:

Fill out this self-evaluation form:

___ **What voices of regret are you listening to?**

___ **What does God say about guilt?**

___ **Are you seated with Christ above Satan or are you wallowing beneath Satan's lies of guilt and condemnation?**

___ **What scripture will you use to combat sin and condemnation?**

FORGIVE
TO FORGET

Chapter 12

If there were but one primary step or key to moving forward in life it would have to be forgiveness. It's easy to say but harder to actually do. Many people will say they have forgiven because they have heard it is the right thing to do, but forgiveness is not a feeling. It is a choice that requires corresponding action. All of us have a tendency to excuse our mistakes by blaming someone else. Sometimes we let ourselves also become the object of blame in an attempt to salvage relationships or receive love from a difficult or even toxic relationship.

When our children were small, they would often get into a squabble about a toy or a head-butting match of "he said, she said." As a parent I would hear their trespasses against one another and try to determine the source of the problem. Afterward, it was necessary to require the offending child or children to apologize for their transgressions. Oftentimes it was a process to get them to admit their wrong actions and to sincerely be sorrowful. On the other side of the equation, we taught the person who had been the recipient of the offense to say, "I forgive you." Then we asked them to follow up with the corresponding action of hugging each other. If they couldn't hug, we knew someone was holding back. And it was easy to tell which child was either not truly sorry or had not forgiven and released the offense to God.

Jesus told us to pray, "And forgive us our sins, as we have forgiven those who sin against us." (Matthew 6:12, NLT) Then He goes on to say, "And don't let us yield to temptation." I believe the two are certainly related. If we don't truly forgive others, we will certainly be led into temptation—guaranteed! We will be tempted to retaliate against them and to take actions in our own hands. The action will be sinful! It will be anger and bitterness turned into division, slander and perhaps physical or financial retribution. Many people are serving a prison sentence today because of the hurt and fury they unleashed.

We are instructed in scripture to feed our enemies and do good to those who mistreat us. Why? It is a sure sign we have no unforgiveness toward them! We are no longer held captive by their actions because we have chosen a higher law—the law of love—and against love there is no law (Ephesians 5:22-23). When we choose to forgive, we are set free from the prison that others' sinful actions were intended to build around our heart . But how do we forgive?

How do we process hurts and our corresponding anger to keep wounds from controlling our lives? Maybe you are the one you haven't forgiven! Perhaps you made decisions and are blaming yourself for yesterday's mistakes. Insecurity and blame could be holding you in a prison of your own making. How do we get free from our own transgressions and those of others? We must manage our thoughts and emotions!

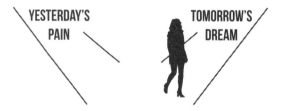

PATH TO FORGIVENESS

Forgive yesterday - It's a choice
THINK FORWARD

YESTERDAY'S PAIN   TOMORROW'S DREAM

The Forgiving Process: Letting Go

You may ask, "How do I manage yesterday's hurts, my mistakes, insecurities, worries and fears?" I'm glad you asked! Take a detour. If you knew a road was taking you off a cliff, you would take a detour, right? Forgiveness is the detour that keeps you from taking the same pathway to regret over and over again. It gives us the ability to let go of yesterday and get on the right path. Forgiveness is a choice! The same Word that paints a picture of who we are, what we have and what we can do calls us out of regret, fear, worry and unresolved hurt. We still have to make the choice daily, but it gets easier when we have programmed our heart and renewed our mind to God's Word.

HOW TO FORGIVE

When we get hurt, we see ourselves as the victim. We feel upset, confused, angry, discouraged, and possibly depressed or suicidal depending on the person and the situation. When someone hurts us, our human nature tells us to get even. If we're upset with ourselves, we may try to get even by inflicting self-harm (e.g., addictions, cutting, sabotaging relationships or sabotaging success).

PAYBACKS

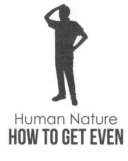  

Human Nature
HOW TO GET EVEN

Offender
TRESPASSER

God's Nature
FORGIVENESS!

Are you angry with yourself? Was there somebody who offended you, betrayed your trust, or broke your heart? You have probably pictured this person and rehearsed what they did to you multiple times, whether it was a recent offense or a long-ago transgression. Perhaps you have already rehearsed how you would get even time and time again. Maybe you have done many things in life to punish this person, but you were ultimately the one held in "time out," disconnecting from life and love. It's time to settle the score! To get even! You heard me! Let's fix this thing once and for all!

Settling the Score

Picture yourself standing face to face with the person who wounded, rejected, stole from or hurt you.

Do you see a thief? A murderer? An abuser? What do you want to do to get even? Let yourself go there for a minute! What do you want to do to them to get even? Yell profane things at them? Slap them? Hit them? Shoot them? Reject them the way they rejected you? Whatever it is you wish you could do, I want you to get that in your mind. You are standing there face to face with your victimizer and it's time to finally settle the score. You have it in your power to harm them or hurt them the way they hurt you. Go for it!

Just as you are on the brink of releasing your fury, Jesus Christ steps in front of you, standing between you and the person who has caused you so much pain. Looking into your eyes, He says compassionately to you, "Whatever you want to do to them, do to me, instead. Unleash your hurt on me. I paid for their sins, their offenses and mistakes just as I paid for yours." What do you want to do to me to get even with them for their offenses against you? He waits for your response.

What will you do to Jesus to get even with them? He's waiting. Will you hit him? Beat him? Pull the trigger? Scream or yell obscenities? Will you do anything? Will you carry it out? Will you drop your charge against them and fall into His arms?

He says to you, "Forgive them as I have forgiven you. Turn them over to me. Trust me with this pain. Only I can be trusted to justify and to judge. No man or woman has the righteous standing to make either decision. On the scales of justice, all men and women are guilty. My sacrifice is sufficient for you both."

Drop your weapons. Release your pain and say, "Father, forgive them. I forgive them." Tears of healing may flow, cleansing the soul. "He restores my soul for His name sake."

Sometimes I feel so hurt or angry, I go from words like, "forgive them, Lord," to "smite them, Lord!" A tug of war is going on in my soul. Then I realize how bitter my heart is, and I realize that my actions are no better than theirs, and I am in need of help; I need forgiveness just as badly as they do. I finally break. I drop my vengeance and with a sincere heart say, "Father, forgive them, and forgive me, too. Forgive me as I forgive those who have trespassed against me."

GOD'S NATURE

What do you want to do to get even?

We all need forgiveness. Extending it to others actually helps us receive it for ourselves. Now the record is clean, and you and I have given them to God to let Him choose what is best as their judge and Savior. Love is a choice. Forgiveness is a choice. Because God loved us, He gave Jesus to die for our sins so we could be freed from the sins of yesterday and live free today.

The Forgetting Process: Moving On

Forgetting is the next choice. Even though our mind still remembers, we choose to forget by no longer rehearsing it. We don't replay it anymore. We don't entertain thoughts or allow it to be rekindled emotionally or revisited mentally unless we are still holding on to something we haven't released. When thoughts or wounds try to stir again, we remind ourselves that we chose to forgive and it is now under the blood of Christ. Who can bring a charge against us? We refuse to retry the case. The case was tried and we released them to the judge for His justice. We are released from our wounds and offenses when we stand before Jesus with our own sin before us, and He calls us innocent and free to go as he took our punishment for us. Thus we forgive as we have been forgiven and must make a choice to not go back to an emotional or mental prison with our offense toward a person or ourselves.

Forgiveness is an act of faith. We forgive ourselves and others by faith in the sacrifice of Jesus. You may ask, "How long do we continue to remind ourselves, and say that it's under the blood of Christ and no longer our pain to carry or burden to punish? Until the day it no longer has any hold on us. At that point, we may speak about it in generalities or stories to help another victim of unforgiveness because it doesn't have the emotional sting anymore. There may be a scar but the healing has occurred and we are free! Where there is much forgiven, there is much love. You and I have been forgiven, and when we remember His sacrifice of love for us, that is enough to keep us whole.

LOVE
ENCOUNTER

Chapter 13

A lady wrote to me and said, "Throughout my life I've been through heartache, and mental and physical pain from the ones who say they love me the most. After 32 years I still carry this heavy burden and as I age, and this weight increases, I find myself continuing to hurt people around me because I feel they're out to hurt me. My husband of nine years has grown further and further away from me. I try to stay and not leave because I fear being alone like my mom and grandma."

This letter reflects the common emotional state of so many, where deep hurts in the emotional realm hold people captive and often result in physical health problems as well. If we allow disappointments from people, who we think will love us, to fester and harden our hearts, emotional heartache and pain can become our constant companions. This lady's struggle started when she was a child, in the same way most of our hurts started. Someone abused us, rejected us, used us or misunderstood us, and we took on those wounds as a part of our identity. We carried them through life and put up walls to avoid being hurt again. We can't love other people while running from relationships and trying to escape from situations that are going to cause us pain, anguish or hurt.

There was a study done by Harvard to unearth the secrets to a happy and purposeful life. In that study, 268 male Harvard undergraduates from the class of 1938 to 1940 were observed for 75 years. A tremendous amount of data was collected on what they did in their lives—their career success, relationship success, and even their heartbreaks and setbacks—to determine what matters the most in life. With nearly a decade of life experiences under their belts, these men came to a unanimous conclusion. "Love is really all that matters," they said. Love. At the end of the day, after their tremendous careers and years of noteworthy accomplishments, the men put the highest value on having love in their lives. And for those who didn't make time for love, that was their biggest regret.

Many of the men had been through the worst and the best of situations. One of the respondents had been suicidal and had endured tremendous trauma early in life, but when they scored him at the end of the 75 years, he actually ranked as one of the highest in happiness and satisfaction. Why? He pursued many things he thought would make him happy in the beginning, chasing after a career and financial success, but he recognized that what he was really longing for was love. He went on a search to find love, and when he found it, his life was radically changed.

The second conclusion the study came to was that the happiest and most fulfilled men found a way of dealing with the stresses of life without pushing love away. Having love in your life, and the ability to receive and give love are the combination for happiness! God created us for love. If we can't connect with others because we put up walls or we're afraid to love, give, be ourselves or be free and vulnerable in a relationship, our happiness and success will be hindered.

The journey from immaturity to maturity is a movement from self-focus on our pain to connection with others and discovering how we can love in spite of the imperfections in all of us. Originally, these Harvard men thought it was all about self-ambition, their career and financial success, but what they realized is that it's about connection. You were made for love; you were made to connect with others.

You can love. I don't care what's happened to you;

I don't care what you've been through in the past; you *can* love. It's a two-way street: we all need to receive love, and we all need to give love. We can't focus on one and neglect the other.

The most difficult funeral I ever attended was for a newborn baby born to a teenage girl who grew up in an extremely dysfunctional family. The baby's nurses said the infant died from neglect. The mother didn't want the baby, so she essentially abandoned it at the hospital. This young woman had not received real love in her life and couldn't give it to her child. I'm not sure she truly understood the choices she made before her child's life was gone. Satan did what he always does after he convinces us to make a mistake. He berated her with guilt, condemnation and regret, pushing her even farther from God. Satan convinces us to sin and when we do, he turns around and tries to get us to plunge into condemnation. Guilt and regret then move into our heart, hardening it and leaving no room for love. The cycle continues to perpetuate unless there is a love encounter that changes the heart. If we fall for the first trick, we can't let ourselves fall for the second. Don't let condemnation keep you from God's free gift of love.

Are Your Expectations Realistic?

Part of the problem is that we go into relationships without understanding that love is not a "feeling," although we can feel love. The feeling of love is the overflow of our *choice* to love.

Ninety-percent of songs are written about love. Perhaps you remember hearing some of these hits on the radio:

> *"What the World Needs Now is Love"* by Jackie DeShannon
>
> *"All You Need is Love"* by The Beatles
>
> *"I Just Called to Say I Love You"* by Stevie Wonder
>
> *"Love Will Keep Us Together"* by Captain & Tenille

Love is what everyone's talking about, and yet nobody has a clue how to find it, maintain it or enjoy it *without* being devastated by it. When someone says, "I love you," they are usually referring to what I call *tabloid love*. Tabloid love is a surface-deep feeling that looks good and feels good. It's like the celebrity couples that look like they have it all together—because she's hot and he's good-looking, they must be the perfect couple. They'll report in the tabloids it's a marriage "made in heaven," but it's not many years later you hear about their nasty divorce. Now they loathe each other, and they're spending millions of dollars fighting in court. The world's definition of love fits better under another word—lust. Lust wants to get something from a person more than it wants to give something to a person. Here's the key: Lust is *selfish*; love is *selfless*.

Step 11: *Love is a choice and you can love anyone, but choose wisely in relationships, or love can turn to hate.*

Lust only lasts for a short while, and then it can quickly turn to hate. Opposites attract, and then they attack. Growing up, there was a couple in our neighborhood that all the women in the community admired. The husband was a psychiatrist, and he would walk arm-in-arm with his wife around the block every evening. He was a good-looking man and seemed so attentive to his wife, all of the other women would jealously watch from their windows, comparing their husband to the handsome psychiatrist.

We saw them together less and less, and soon news leaked that the psychiatrist was divorcing his wife and leaving her for another woman. I looked at the situation and thought, "Wow! It looked and felt like love, but appearances can be deceptive." Be careful for what the world thinks is love!

God's love is *agape* love, and it seeks the best for a person's life. When a relationship is built on agape love, both people are trying to get something *to* the other person instead of trying to get something *from* them. Agape love isn't narcissistic, or all about "my desires" or "my needs." That kind of love hurts, damages and wounds people. And all too often, hurting people hurt other people. You can say you love someone, but it's not really love until there are difficult situations to endure together. Agape love is an unconditional commitment to an imperfect person. There are no perfect people or relationships, but great relationships are built from the foundation of agape love— God's Love.

Statistically, second marriages have less of a chance at success, and the numbers decline even further in third and fourth marriages. Why? Too often the wounds that undermined the previous marriage are carried into the next. People think they're going to find greener grass somewhere else, yet often they just start all over with a new set of problems. Instead of pushing love away, I always tell people maybe it would be best to invest in the marriage you are in. A new person isn't going to change you, the inner turmoil or the emptiness. Maybe a new you, renewed thoughts and a new way of approaching life is the best answer. Our goal should be to love like God does. His standard and Word is perfect, but when we fall short of the good plan He has, His love is still always there for us, cheering us to get back up.

The Insecurity Cover-Up: "Fighting" vs. "Hiding"

My husband and I came from very different family backgrounds, and we learned to deal with our emotions in different ways. Growing up I developed a "perform for love" mentality. I always felt like I had to do more to gain approval from my family and friends. I was hungry for praise and searching for identity. I was trying to answer the questions, *"Am I valuable? Am I accepted? Am I loved?"* Children are born looking for identity.

My husband struggled with fear of failure and

rejection as well, but his way of handling it was to shy away from the risk of failure. He wanted to hide from life. We were on different sides of the ditch, but we were both in a ditch, nonetheless. We merely expressed our insecurities in different ways. Many people allow insecurities to drive them into these two ditches:

On one hand, there are the people who want to hide from the risk, from the judgment and from the possibility of failure. This side of the ditch says, "I'm going to quit before I even try; that way I don't look bad. I'm not worthy of love."

On the other hand, there are the people who try to earn love through work, popularity and relationships. This side of the ditch says, "I'm going to prove that I'm loveable through my actions. And if anyone thinks otherwise, I'll show them."

Gary's and my different ways of handling pressure caused a lot of conflict in the early years of our marriage until we learned that our identity and love came from God. By receiving His love, we had the ability to love each other. But we had to choose to believe that the other one was committed whether either of us could show it or say it properly. I had to start saying to myself, "I know his heart. Even if he's not saying it how I would, or acting how I would, his heart is still toward me. That's his way of expressing himself." He might have had a rough day, or he might be dealing with a difficult situation, but he loves me. And more importantly, I am loved.

God doesn't just choose to love you and me; He is love. God is love, and He sent His Son Jesus to die for us all. When we were unlovely, broken, messed up and confused, God chose to love us. He saw our confusion and He understood. We didn't have anything to offer God except our brokenness, but He chose to love us and make something beautiful from our brokenness. That's what God's love can do in our lives. It doesn't matter where we came from or the brokenness, the pain, the messed up situations we've been in or how many people we've hurt, God loves and forgives us. It's His nature. He is love.

Step 12: *Recognize that everyone has shortcomings, but that doesn't make you unlovable.*

The apostle Paul, zealous for the law, persecuted and murdered Christians. He justified himself by his works and judged others who didn't measure up to his performance. When our love is based on performance, we judge others, and the same way we judge is the way it comes back to us. A critical spirit is hard to bear, and people become critical when they shut love out and find fault with others by pushing them away.

The Left Ditch: Unworthiness

The mantra of the left ditch is, *"I can't, so I won't even try."* Unworthiness drives people to pull away from relationships, possibility, and ultimately, life. If I hide because I don't want to fail, then I've failed already.

Growing up, Gary would hide when company came over. He was painfully shy. After being bullied as a little boy, he was afraid of rejection. There was anger in his home, and as the oldest, his father took it out on him. His dream was to escape to the mountains to live in a log cabin, away from the world so he wouldn't have to deal with people. God sure has a sense of humor! God gave him a talkative, ambitious wife instead. I remember when we first got married he told me, "We'll just live in a log cabin, and we'll probably never amount to much, but we'll be happy with our love."

"Oh no we're not!" I said. I knew he had a call of God on his life. Behind every great man of God is a woman who's praying, encouraging, and at times, biting her tongue.

Hiding our problems and hiding from the people who can recognize them seem like the easiest options at times. We think the closer people get, the more of our failure they'll see. And that's true. People will see our failure, but where we're wrong is thinking that's a bad thing. The fact is, no matter what side of the ditch we're on, we all fall short of the glory of Jesus. The beauty isn't in our perfection but in the way Jesus turns our brokenness into *His* perfection. We can never reach the place God wants us to be if we are weighted down by unworthiness.

God Can't Heal What We Hide

When we are wrong it's easy to justify our actions instead of admitting our wrongs and receiving restoration. There's a saying, "God cannot heal what we hide." Oftentimes the world is trying to justify sin and wrongdoing, thinking it will make them feel better while the church world is judging people by God's standard and condemning them. The Bible says Jesus didn't come to the earth to condemn it but that it might be saved (John 3:17). The truth is none of us can live up to God's perfect way or His right ways without HIM. After the choice that Adam and Eve made to rebel against God's plan, mankind has been living in the vicious cycle of brokenness, justifying and judging, falling and failing. When we receive God's love to cleanse us from all sin and error, we must also receive His grace to walk in the light. Our faith is a life-long learning and growing process, walking out our new life in Christ not just in spirit but also in soul and body.

There are women who think, "Ah, it would be awesome to be married to Gary (or some other man of God)." I've had women say, "Do you just sit at his feet and he feeds you the Word of God all day long?"

Ha!

The reality is we have to work at our marriage just like you do! We have flesh and a will, and sometimes it's aligned with God's will, and sometimes we have to check our hearts and choose to bring our will and attitudes into alignment with God's Word and plan. But we've learned there's a better way than selfishness—the way of love.

I have five children. I love every one of them individually. I may favor the actions of one over the other at a given time, but it doesn't mean I love one of them more than another. My love for them is uniquely theirs. No one can replace the love I have for each one. Because I love them so much, it's very doubtful I would give one of them up to die for someone. I'm sorry! I just love them that much. That is the great love God has for you. He knew you and I could not justify our own sins and He didn't want to judge us so instead He judged our sin and laid it on Jesus to pay the penalty we deserved.

When Jesus was rejected, when he was reviled and they cursed Him and spat on Him, the Bible says He reviled not. In other words He did not return their actions. He did not repeat or do what they did to Him. That's what we tend to do though, right? We get mad at someone and want to get even if they hurt us. The Bible says, "How can you say you love God if you can't love your brother?" And "Love your enemies." How hard is that? But if God was willing to give His own Son to die for each of us, what right do we have to condemn one another or ourselves? Each of us has value and purpose in His plan. He laid down His life for you, so what kind of value do you have? The value is worth what someone is willing to pay. You are extremely valuable.

For the joy that was set before Him, Jesus endured the cross (Hebrews 12:2). What is the joy that was set before Him? It was not sitting at the right hand of God or being declared the King of kings and the Lord of lords. It was bringing us home to Father God as sons and daughters. That was the joy that caused Him to endure a horrific death on the cross and separation from God to bear our sin. So Jesus wasn't looking for power, and He wasn't looking for glory; He was looking to be glorified in those He loves. Love is a choice; love is a decision.

God didn't make us love Him. He didn't say, "You have to love Me." He's not a tyrant. He's not controlling. God gave us the freewill to choose our path. Joshua put it strongly, "But if serving the Lord seems undesirable to you, then choose for yourselves this day whom you will serve…" (Joshua 24:15) You and I can choose love today;

we are free to choose His love. Now if you choose His love, you're accepted into His kingdom. God does not reject you because He doesn't love you. The only rejection we experience is when we reject Him and say no to His love, when we won't receive His love or when we say, "I don't want it, God. No thank you, I'll do it my way." Yet God put value on us in that He loved us when we were yet sinners, or separated from Him by sin (Romans 5:8).

The Right Ditch: Performance

The right ditch says, "I don't need anybody. I can earn my worth." It happens when we've been deeply wounded, and we try to protect ourselves from being wounded again. We begin to try to work for love, people-please and do life in our ability. In school I was the class president, yearbook editor and voted most likely to succeed. I was terrified of rejection. I performed and performed for love, but I never felt satisfied. I became suicidal, because I thought if I've accomplished this much and I still feel this way, I don't want to live. We see the evidence of this mindset rampant in Hollywood. People try to make something of themselves, performing for love and acceptance, but they can never do enough. They've done great things, and accomplished substantial wealth, but then they take their life. They feel like they've arrived, and they're still not satisfied. Money is a disappointing master, and the approval of people is a disappointing reward.

My husband is a very calm man. He doesn't easily get upset or angry. In the early years of our marriage we got into a disagreement, and no matter how Gary tried to console me, I became more angry and more emotional. I yelled, "You don't love me! You don't love me!"

He was so frustrated that he started to laugh. He didn't know what to do! He had tried every word, but nothing could make me happy. If he said he loved me, I didn't believe him. If he said I was beautiful, I didn't believe him. I wanted him to fill something in me that couldn't be filled. I was looking for my identity in him instead of in God's love.

When he started to laugh, I lost it. All of my insecurities shouted, "He's mocking you! He's making fun of you!" I went into a fit of rage—throwing things, crying and slamming doors. I locked myself in our bathroom and refused to open the door. I guess I wanted him to bust it open and *prove* his love to me. Prove that I was worthy. Eventually he surrendered and went to sleep, and as I climbed in bed that night, I determined to make him sleep miserably. I tossed and turned, jabbed him with my elbow and made every effort to show how angry I was.

"If I'm miserable, he's going to be miserable," I thought.

I am ashamed to admit the extent I went to in an effort to find approval. The next morning I was still upset. Gary broke down in tears and said, "Drenda, I love you, but I don't know how I can get it through that thick wall and that thick head of yours and help you see how much I love you." The problem was not in him; it was in me.

God loves you unconditionally, but he can't bless you unconditionally if you keep saying, "No." The Bible says, "If you're willing and obedient, you'll eat the good of the land" (Isaiah 1:19). If you won't invest in others or let others invest in you, or if you won't receive God's love, you can never give love freely. I couldn't return love to my husband if I couldn't receive that he loved me. God's not withholding anything from us, but if I withhold my heart, I can't receive all God wants for me. Stop competing, stop hiding, and let God transform you by His love.

God loves you like you're His little child. He's not looking for performance from you; He just wants you to be His child. We don't mind when our children aren't perfect, do we? When my children brought me a picture they drew, I didn't point out every place it was out of the lines, or scoff at their rendition of a house. To me, it was perfect. I proudly put it on my fridge!

All You Need *Isn't* Love!

The Beatles once sang a song called, "All You Need is Love." Well, that's only partially true. Adam and Eve were in the Garden and they had complete perfect love. They needed something more than love—they needed *truth* and *obedience*. Because they chose to believe a lie and weren't obedient to what God said, they actually shut love out of their life! Sometimes we blame God for things that have gone wrong in our life when they were merely the consequences of our disobedience. We need truth and obedience alongside of love. When Adam and Eve chose to disobey God, they opened the door to shame, guilt, blame, fear, rejection, insecurity and unworthiness. When they chose to sin, they became naked and ashamed. Before the fall they were free to be themselves; they didn't have to cover anything. They didn't have to dress to best accentuate their body type, or make themselves look more important with designer accessories, or cover their imperfections with make-up. They could be themselves and enjoy the freedom of being who God created them to be.

Staying on the Road

In the left ditch there's insecurity, and in the right ditch there's insecurity—the only place where there is security is in Christ! The only way we can be completely free is in Christ. Anything else is a ditch.

If you look at the Word of God, you'll get a picture of what love looks like and how loved you are. You'll get an assurance on the inside of you that's greater than any rejection you've experienced or any voice that says you're unlovable. The world defines who you are by what you have, but they've got it all wrong. You don't get your identity from your performance; you get your performance from your identity!

When who I am is secure in Christ, now whatever anyone else says or doesn't say doesn't define me.

I'm free.

Some people are what I like to call "ditch hoppers." I used to be one! I'd go from the ditch of performing and when I failed, I'd switch over to the ditch of unworthiness. The devil doesn't mind if you're driving from ditch to ditch. The point is you're still in a ditch. You perform, you feel great, you fail, and then you feel like a loser. It's a cycle we fall into—high, low, high, low, high, low. God has a better plan. When you put your eyes on Him you can stay on the road!

Emotion Kick-start Challenge:

___ **Dedicate a whole day to showing somebody you love them through your actions.**

> Experience the joy of giving and observe how they treat you in return. Do you feel more loved when you express love to others?

___ **Treat yourself.**

> Show yourself some appreciation by investing in a new outfit, new hobby or by spending time doing something that you love. Remind yourself why you're awesome (and totally loveable).

___ **Smile at the people you pass by throughout your day.**

> Make it a goal to positively impact as many people's days as you can by sharing a smile with them.

___ **Give ten hugs in one day.**

> Hug the friends and family you meet throughout your day. How does it make you feel? Does it change the way they respond to you? You can set a personal goal number or stick with ten hugs.

YOUR
BETTER
LIFE

Chapter 14

I remember one of our business mentors saying many years ago, "Things are never as bad as you feel or as good as you feel, so be level headed and don't overreact to good or bad news." Speaking from experiential situations, he was right. If we respond to negative news with discouragement and feel like it's useless to go on, we may quit short of seeing the dream in our heart come to pass. We need to remind ourselves it's better than we feel! Our feelings need an anchor. Our soul must be controlled by the Spirit and anchored to God's Word. What did He say? If He said it, I simply must choose to believe it. And when I feel contrary to what He said, I must bring my soul into subjection or make it subject to the Word of God. Feelings change, but God's Word never changes. It stands forever.

Feelings can be fickle and cause us to take the wrong path or response to hardships. On the other hand, when things go well, we can also get ourselves into trouble by presuming on the future. That's exactly what debt does! In business, if we make our first sale and assume that everything will always be easy, we may be tempted to go purchase a Lamborghini when our bank account says we can afford a motor scooter! We can't build our lives successfully around the uncertainty of emotional feelings with their ups and downs and roller coaster moods. We must build our lives around something much more steadfast. "Be steadfast, [unshakable,] immovable, always abounding in the work of the Lord..." (1 Corinthians 15:58 ESV). Those who have success have learned to master their emotions instead of allowing them to master them. The Word of God gives us a renewed mind, and the Holy Spirit empowers us to keep our emotions in control. We need both the picture and the power to succeed and thankfully God has given us both!

Emotions can fuel our purpose and give us the zeal to take action, but they should never be in the driver seat of our lives. We can be angry at injustice and let it fuel us to fight for change, but we can't afford to let our anger turn into sin. If the sun goes down and we are angry, we may develop a negative outlook and become cynical and bitter. We are called to make things better, not bitter! Bitter people don't change things; they become part of the problem. God has given us emotion and feelings to experience intimacy and passion and resolve to love others and make the world a better place. In the hands of the enemy, our emotions can be our undoing. In the hands of God, they became the passion that extends compassion to a hurting person.

A double-minded person is unstable in all their ways. The quickest way to a double-minded life is to let the erratic notion of emotion lead our choices, decisions and actions. A double-minded person will move two steps forward and one step back because they are easily moved off their stand of God's Word by cunning and crafty people, criticism or discouragement. And even success can be our undoing

"Joy is the praise language of God."

if we aren't self-controlled and alert. Satan is seeking an opportunity to attack; but the Bible says to keep yourself, and the wicked one touches you not. (See 1 John 5:18.) This conveys that the wicked one is often given place in our lives because we are drawn into emotional situations and reactions that move us away from God's choices for our life, including His love and protection. Give no place to the devil. There's no room in your life to let him take up residence.

Joy is the praise language of God. When we choose to rejoice regardless of how we feel, the garment of praise will lift us out of discouragement and feelings of hopelessness.

Remember Paul and Silas praised God in a jail cell, and their faith to praise God within the painful situation, created an explosive reaction of the earth and resulted in their chains falling off and freedom from captivity as the jail door was opened too. First, joy and praising God changed them and their outlook, then it broke chains or things off of them, and then it changed things around them. In the same way, joy strengthens us in situations and brings the power of God, chasing sorrow away. Sometimes we need to remind ourselves, "This too shall pass!" David said (more than once), "I will again praise God!" God didn't create the problem, but He is the answer.

God doesn't tempt us with evil. The Bible says to let no man say that God tempted Him, but each of us is drawn off by our own lusts into sin. (See James 13-15.) Some of these lusts are very subtle, like the lust to be right and prove it, or to get the most attention, accolades, money or power over others. We can covet or lust after something a friend has and become offended that we don't. We can become critical of others because secretly we envy their position or influence. Honestly, if we understood the price or the responsibility, we would be much more gracious with others and less critical of their performance. Leadership and business ownership are exacting and often require years of sacrifice and development, which are not obvious to the bystander once success is realized. There's a joke that self-employed people work 80 hours a week not to have to work 40!

Determine to be your personal best and to learn from many successful people how they did it. Once you experience success, realize there is no less responsibility, but actually there will be more because of your achievement. But it's worth it! Ultimately only God and His Word can help us navigate through the various prices and pressures of life, leadership and monetary gain. We can't skip character development or discipline, or any success we have will be short-lived.

It is better than you feel if you are in a battle against depression or discouragement. It is better than you feel if you are lonely from divorce or abandonment. It is better than you feel if the doctor gives you a bad report and says he has no hope for you. It is better than you feel if you are missing out on an invitation to be among the "who's who" because you stand for something others reject. It's better than you feel if your bank account is empty and your wallet is flat.

How can it be better than you feel? Feelings have nothing to do with your potential! God's Word is better than your feelings. God's truth is more real than the circumstance. It is possible to stand even when you don't "feel" like it. Sometimes we have to speak to ourselves and the circumstance, and tell our soul to submit when things don't feel good. Our flesh likes comfort but comfort isn't the goal—victory is! There is no victory without doing some uncomfortable things! But it is worth it! This light and momentary affliction or situation is working for you a far more glorious future if you will only believe. (See 2 Corinthians 4:17.) We aren't to stay in the affliction; there's no glory in that, but rather to stand in it and patiently let God work it out. Trust is required to know that He is working things out regardless of how we feel. Feelings can lie, but God cannot! We choose to put on the garment of praise for the spirit of heaviness and lift up our voice to God.

Choose to fight with spiritual weapons and God's Word, and at the end of the fight, you'll still be standing. When you do all that you know to do, and it still isn't looking good, don't be moved into feelings of self-pity or offense; instead be moved only by truth, and it *will* move mountains.

Believe what God believes and speak what God says, and your feelings will soon follow your faith. This is our confidence: if we ask anything according to His Word, we know He hears us and if He hears us we know, we have those things we desired of Him. (See 1 John 5:14-15.) Confidence in God's Word will not disappoint us.

If your life feels like a movie and you're in the middle of a cliffhanger, don't be moved. The story isn't finished, and the plot is still unfolding. You may only be seeing the difficult part of the story, but it has a good ending with God's Word as the storyteller. The only reason it wouldn't end well is if we aren't willing to finish the story with Him as the writer and the spirit of faith as the publisher.

Jesus paid the ransom for all things that pertain to life and godliness. Choose today to take the steps to renew your mind, possess and control your soul, and submit your will to God. Then your spirit, soul and body will be found blameless at the coming of our Lord Jesus Christ; and your life will exemplify His mark of the high calling. This is your better life! Take charge of it with God's help. It's your time to move into your destiny!

Emotional Healing:
Psalm 147:3 (NIV)
> *He heals the brokenhearted and binds up their wounds.*

Building Trust:
Proverbs 29:25 (NIV)
> *Fear of man will prove to be a snare, but whoever trusts in the Lord is kept safe.*

Galatians 1:10 (NIV)
> *Am I now trying to win the approval of human beings, or of God? Or am I trying to please people? If I were still trying to please people, I would not be a servant of Christ.*

Dealing with Anger:
Ephesians 4:31-32 (NIV)
> *Get rid of all bitterness, rage and anger, brawling and slander, along with every form of malice. Be kind and compassionate to one another, forgiving each other, just as in Christ God forgave you.*

Proverbs 17:27 (NIV)
> *The one who has knowledge uses words with restraint, and whoever has understanding is even-tempered.*

Developing a teachable spirit:
Proverbs 19:20 (NIV)
> *Listen to advice and accept discipline, and at the end you will be counted among the wise.*

Matthew 18:15 (NIV)
> *If your brother or sister sins, go and point out their fault, just between the two of you. If they listen to you, you have won them over.*

Living a life of Love:
Matthew 22:36-39 (NLT)
> *Jesus replied, "'You must love the Lord your God with all your heart, all your soul, and all your mind.' This is the first and greatest commandment. A second is equally important: 'Love your neighbor as yourself.'*

Proverbs 10:12 (NIV)
> *Hatred stirs up conflict, but love covers over all wrongs.*

Avoiding abusive relationships:

Proverbs 22:24 (NIV)

Do not make friends with a hot-tempered person, do not associate with one easily angered.

Guarding your heart:

Proverbs 4:23 (NIV)

Above all else, guard your heart, for everything you do flows from it.

Matthew 12:34 (AMP)

For the mouth speaks out of that which fills the heart. The good man, from his [inner] good treasure, brings out good things; and the evil man, from his [inner] evil treasure, brings out evil things.

No Fear:

Romans 8:15 (NIV)

The Spirit you received does not make you slaves, so that you live in fear again; rather, the Spirit you received brought about your adoption to sonship. And by him we cry, "Abba, Father."

Offenses:

James 5:16 (AMP)

Therefore, confess your sins to one another [your false steps, your offenses], and pray for one another, that you may be healed and restored. The heartfelt and persistent prayer of a righteous man (believer) can accomplish much [when put into action and made effective by God—it is dynamic and can have tremendous power].

Proverbs 17:9 (NIV)

Whoever would foster love covers over an offense, but whoever repeats the matter separates close friends.

Self-control:

Proverbs 16:32 (NIV)

Better a patient person than a warrior, one with self-control than one who takes a city.

1 Corinthians 9:25 (AMP)

Now every athlete who [goes into training and] competes in the games is disciplined and exercises self-control in all things. They do it to win a crown that withers, but we [do it to receive] an imperishable [crown that cannot wither].

GOD DIDN'T DESIGN YOU TO FAIL!